YOU MIGHT BE A NARCISSIST IF....

How to Identify Narcissism in Ourselves and Others and What We Can Do About It

YOU MIGHT BE A NARCISSIST IF....

How to Identify Narcissism in Ourselves and Others and What We Can Do About It

Paul Meier, M.D.
Lisa Charlebois, L.C.S.W.
Cynthia Munz, L.M.F.T.

Langdon Street Press
212 3rd Avenue North, Suite 290
Minneapolis, MN 55401
612.455.2293
www.langdonstreetpress.com

ISBN - 978-1-934938-74-4
ISBN - 1-934938-74-2
LCCN - 2009936253

Book sales for North America and international:
Itasca Books, 3501 Highway 100 South, Suite 220
Minneapolis, MN 55416
Phone: 952.345.4488 (toll free 1.800.901.3480)
Fax: 952.920.0541; email to orders@itascabooks.com

Cover Design by Madge Duffy
Typeset by James Arneson

Printed in the United States of America

LANGDON
STREET
PRESS

Table of Contents

To my husband Danny,
Thank you for loving me enough to confront me with the truth about my own narcissism. I am grateful that you have done so with such grace, compassion, endless love, and patience so that I can bear it. Thank you for showing me what real love is. This book would never have been possible without you.

Lisa

To my husband Eric,
I have you in my heart.

Cynthia

ACKNOWLEDGEMENTS

Lisa Charlebois

I first want to thank my clients, because this book would never have been written if you hadn't continually urged me to put what I say "into a book so it can help others." I also want to thank my husband, Danny, and my three teens, Danielle, Derek, and Travis, who have been wholeheartedly supportive of this endeavor even though it has taken my time away from them. I also want to thank my friends, other family members, and colleagues who have continually expressed their total confidence that my dream would become a reality.

In addition, I want to express my gratitude to my previous therapist, Cathryn Campbell, whose empathy for my woundedness taught me empathy for myself, which increased my capacity for empathy with others. I also want to thank my mentors, Stephen Tuttle, Dr. John Townsend, and Dr. Henry Cloud. Your insights and teachings helped shape my thoughts and understanding so I could redefine for myself what it means to be human. This has created great growth in me both personally and professionally and has made me a better person and therapist. Finally, I am grateful to my husband, Danny, for all the getaways you took me on so I could write, and to my two writing partners, Paul and Cynthia. This book would have never been possible without the three of you.

Cynthia Munz

I want to express my deep gratitude to all of our clients who have put their trust in us to get this message out. I also want to sincerely thank my mentors Gretchen Morgan and Stephen Tuttle. You have helped me to uncover my weaknesses and to find my heart, and, in the process, to discover my life's message. I will forever be grateful to you. And to you, Lisa, for all the hours we spent together…for your honesty and transparency…I have grown as a person.

Introduction to Narcissism Awareness

Narcissists are basically people who think the world revolves around them (or if it doesn't, it should!). I (Paul) am a psychiatrist who has treated hundreds of people with this personality trait and thousands who have been negatively impacted by narcissists. In 1993, I appeared on the *Oprah Winfrey* show to discuss a book I had written about narcissists called *Don't Let Jerks Get the Best of You*, and another book on codependency (about being addicted to having narcissistic friends or mates) called *Love Is a Choice*. In reality, we all have a few of these narcissistic tendencies.

For many years, I have felt a strong need to write a serious psychological book about the causes and cures of narcissism and how to protect ourselves from narcissists. I have known and worked with one of my editors over the years, so she knows that I, like most authors, have a few of these narcissistic traits. So I asked her jokingly, "What do you want me to call the book, *Narcissism and How I Attained It?*" I told her it could consist of three hundred pictures of me along with a two-page autobiography. She laughed and said, "Paul, just try to recall any people you have come across in your life and career who are more narcissistic than you are and write about them!" I told her I thought I could do that.

A few years ago, I enjoyed a TV special based on the *New York Times* bestseller *You Might Be a Redneck If....* So, shortly after that, some friends of mine and I jokingly and spontaneously thought of some ideas for "You might be a narcissist if..." We took turns making up one liners about narcissistic behaviors we have observed in people over the years (including ourselves!). It created a more lighthearted avenue to confront each other on our own narcissistic traits. In fact, one night, I was supposed to pick up my friends at 6:00 p.m. for a ride to the restaurant where we had reservations, and I was so absorbed with writing material for this narcissism book that I lost track of time and was late. So, my buddy made me promise to add, "You might be a narcissist if you are so busy writing a book on narcissism that you forget to pick up your friends on time for a dinner date!" I hope this book will help us all see narcissism more clearly in others and ourselves.

At the same time, we do not want to make light of the serious devastation narcissists have inflicted on millions of people throughout history, including now, all around the world. We continually see numerous lives, marriages, families, even churches torn apart from the destructive forces of narcissism.

However, what we know to be true is that it is a rare person who intentionally sets out to destroy his[1] own life or the lives of the people he loves. But until we each become more conscious of which attitudes, feelings, and behaviors inadvertently hurt ourselves or others, we tend to go on for years repeating the same patterns, communicating in the same ways, not setting healthy boundaries, and so on. Life can become utterly frustrating and exhausting!

When we know what the issues are, we can change. Some of us will take longer than others to change, and some of us will need therapy to change, but we all *can* change. It is invigorating to know that we don't have to stay stuck, even if we're not struggling with narcissism. We can change the way we relate to the people who do struggle. Narcissistic character traits are very common. What we have come to see is that the more we are able to recognize and address these characteristics, the more we become truly free to love others as we love ourselves in healthy ways.

Over the years, we have found that many of our clients grew up in narcissistic homes. They don't know that they did. They don't know what is wrong with their lives. They initially don't realize that they have continued to fill their lives with other narcissists,

---

1. Throughout the book, we will randomly make references to both male and female genders; in each case, the statement or example applies to both genders.

and this is why, no matter how hard they try, their relationships aren't working. It's because they haven't known what they're dealing with.

The great joy we have in our jobs is that once people can recognize the truth, they can begin to first get healthier themselves and then learn how to set healthier boundaries with others and initiate relationships with healthier people. These safer relationships provide them with the emotional energy they need in order to interact with the narcissists in their lives.

Our hope is that this book will put words to people's experiences. In fact, that is why our clients have urged us to put our thoughts into writing. As they heal, they come across so many others who are struggling with the same issues.

We are grateful that our clients have let us share some of their stories with you. We have, of course, changed their names and identifying information, but we believe that their thoughts, feelings, attitudes, and experiences relating to narcissism will help us all be able to see the issue at hand more clearly. Let us begin.

CHAPTER 1

SO, WHAT EXACTLY IS NARCISSISM?

I (Lisa) remember when I first got married and suddenly my husband, Danny, and I both came face to face with my narcissistic parts. Who would have thought? Certainly not me! It was 1986. I had graduated the year before with my Bachelor's in Psychology. I was getting ready to begin graduate work so that I could become a psychotherapist. I believed that I was the picture of mental and emotional health (hear the grandiosity?). Sure, I had had my issues earlier in life, but I had seen a psychologist for about eight sessions when I was fifteen. He released me from therapy saying that I had no more issues to work on (unfortunately, he bought the false self-image I had been creating to hide my pain and insecurity).

I had built a lot of friendships throughout my college years. I had great communication skills (or so I thought) and felt I was quite insightful and, quite frankly, I thought Danny was getting a pretty good deal! Truly, if I had known how much suffering I was about to put him through during the ensuing years, I would have rather spared him the agony. (Selfishly, for me, I'm glad I didn't know).

Here we were, married, and we had moved away from our support system so I could attend graduate school. First of all, I was shocked by how much anxiety I had about having my house look perfect. If it didn't look like an immaculately cleaned hotel room that no one was yet staying in, I felt overwhelmed with shame and was sure I would be judged as bad and worthless. Therefore, I suddenly turned into a hypercritical wife if Danny left an article of clothing on the floor (so that it looked as if someone was actually living there), and my thoughts would yell out in my head, "What is he doing? He's wrecking my world! What a pig!" I have to admit that I was rather shocked myself to hear my internal dialogue, because my college roommates would agree that I certainly was not a perfectionist when I lived with them.

Then, if Danny ever dared to give *me* feedback or express that he didn't like something that I had done—if he felt I had been selfish, which I was, or he felt I was being too critical of him, which I was, or he felt I wasn't communicating my feelings clearly because I tended to convert hurt or fear into anger and then attack him with rage, which I did (you get the picture)—I would immediately become defensive, would deny any fault or responsibility, and would then, in fact, turn the conversation around and blame *him*!

I used a ton of projection, which means that *I accused him of the very things I was doing* (although it was unconscious—not in my awareness—so I denied it whenever he tried to point that out). Pretty crazy.... But that's all typical when you're interacting with someone who is narcissistic or is narcissistically defended.

In response, Danny did what healthy people tend to do when someone accuses them of something. Healthy people will stop and take a look at themselves to see if they might have misunderstood something and perhaps unknowingly did what the other person is accusing them of. Then, if they discover that they even unintentionally hurt the other person, they will apologize for the pain they accidentally created. Their empathy for the other's hurt feelings helps to mend the temporary break in the relationship.

This is exactly what Danny would do. After I had turned the entire conversation around and blamed him for how *he* had, in fact, wounded *me,* he would apologize; I would lick my wounds, and eventually, when *I* came around to forgiving *him,* we would make up.

It took some time before Danny was able to see this insidious pattern. Then, one day, he came to me and said, "Honey, now that we've been married for a year, something has recently occurred to me that I wanted to share with you. I know I've made a lot of mistakes during our first year of marriage and have had a lot to learn, and I know I've probably had to apologize for something just about every day. Would you agree with that?" I, of course, agreed, but started to get slightly anxious. He proceeded with, "Well, what recently occurred to me is that I can't think of a time when you've ever said you were sorry to me for anything." His tone of voice remained loving yet genuinely perplexed while he continued with, "I'm just not sure how that can be possible…. I mean, we're both human, and that's part of being human—that we won't be right all the time and everyone makes mistakes. Right?"

Well, how could I argue with that? For the first time, I became aware that I was behaving that way. I was astounded, and my first thought was, "And I'm going to be a therapist?" I vowed to try to become more aware of my behavior and to make healthy changes. And this is when life became very difficult for me!

I wouldn't have thought this would be so hard. Here is what I set out to do: 1) Listen when the other person speaks, 2) express empathy for his feelings, and 3) apologize for hurting him (even if you hurt him unintentionally). After all, this is what I expected from Danny, and this is what he did. We always worked things out, and I always felt so much better because he conveyed he cared about my feelings. Surely, I could do the same thing. Right? Especially because I was learning healthy communication skills in graduate school. Right? Wrong!

I became aware of the disturbing fact that whenever Danny gave me feedback about myself, suggesting that I was less than perfect, I suddenly became filled with panic. If I tried to acknowledge (even if only inside myself) the truth in his feedback, I was filled with dread and then shame, and that soon turned into self-loathing and eventually self-hatred. My feelings would become so intolerable that I would then have to project them back onto Danny and would tell him that *he* was the cause of *my* behavior so that it was all, in fact, *his* fault and *not mine*!

I'll never forget the day when he simply stated, "You know? You could just say you are sorry!" I yelled, "What?" He said, "You could just apologize for hurting my feelings, even if you didn't mean to, and I would feel better and then we could go on with our day." I said, "Really?" This is when I became more conscious of my narcissistic fears. I was afraid that if I admitted fault, it would be seen as weakness, which would then be used against me. I was afraid I would be humiliated and shamed, overexposed. To be vulnerable and human meant death to me!

I couldn't quite believe Danny's words, yet I knew him to be kind and forgiving and to not expect perfection from himself or others. What a concept! Why did I not know how to do this? I then knew I needed to get into my own therapy, and that's exactly what I did.

I wish I could say that character changes don't take long. I wish I could say that I was "cured" in six months. No, what I came to learn about character change is that it is a slow process of relearning what it means to be human, what it means to love and to take in love, what it means to become healthily attached, that it is okay to need. I had to learn empathy for myself by taking in my therapist's empathy for my woundedness before I could truly have empathy in my closest relationships when I hurt the ones I loved. I had to learn to accept myself for who I am—strengths, weaknesses, and all. I was able to do this after experiencing my therapist's true acceptance of me even though I shared with her my inadequacies, my darkest parts, and my deepest shame.

We are writing this book because, as in my (Lisa's) case, narcissism is commonly and unknowingly the cause of a lot of relational frustration and pain. It is likely that you or someone you love (or are trying to love—or tried to love in the past!) is struggling with narcissism. The term narcissism is used frequently in our society, yet it is often misused and often misunderstood.

Overt Narcissism

Much of the literature written on the subject of narcissism describes the overt narcissist, the blatant, bragging, obnoxious, haughty person who completely lacks empathy for others. This type and degree of narcissism is found in only a small percentage of people. What we see and hear about much more often is covert narcissism (also called the inverted narcissist, but we think covert is a clearer term).

Covert Narcissism

The covert narcissist is much shyer and is only quietly grandiose. This person actually often avoids being in the spotlight, although she tends to move up ladders quickly as she gains the confidence and admiration of others with her extreme self-confidence. This narcissist has much better social skills than the overt narcissist, and it is usually only the people closest to her who see that she often lacks self-confidence and is prone to anxiety, depression, and moodiness. She often feels that she is being neglected by others or that they have intentionally slighted her or are persecuting her, when, in reality, they're not.

What you will find much more noticeable about this narcissist is that she is quietly grandiose. You somehow get that she is always right. She needs things to go her way. She will often show resistance to other people's ideas and will give the impression that she doesn't think their ideas are as good as her own, although, sometimes, her disregard of others' opinions will be far less obvious. She'll feign consideration of their ideas and will then simply go on with her plans without considering altering her course. Her confidence can seem unshakable so, often, others come to assume she must be right. I (Lisa) know that I totally came across like this early on in my marriage to Danny!

More traits of the covert narcissist will become rather glaring in the following case example:

Colette and Andrea

Colette came into therapy saying that she wanted to learn more about her own character because a close, four-year friendship with her pastor's wife, Andrea, had just suddenly ended, and Andrea was no longer even speaking to her. Colette was devastated. After replaying the sequence of events over and over in her head (day and night), she still couldn't figure out what had gone wrong, so she decided to seek professional advice.

Here's how the story unfolded. Colette, who was married and had four young children, had been volunteering countless hours each week at the church office helping Andrea with women's ministry events. Recently, Colette asked Andrea if they could meet, and at the meeting Colette expressed that she felt she needed to decrease her volunteer hours so she could focus more on her family, because she was feeling stressed out and overwhelmed. Colette recalled that as she was expressing her feelings to Andrea, it suddenly felt as though the air grew cold in Andrea's office. Colette could feel Andrea emotionally withdraw from her, so she asked Andrea if she was angry about Colette wanting to decrease her hours. Andrea coldly replied, while chuckling sarcastically, "Of course not! Why would I be angry that *you* need to get *your* priorities straight?"

Upon hearing Andrea's tone of voice, Colette suddenly felt chastised, ashamed, and stupid. She felt the utter weight of what a huge disappointment she was to Andrea. She would have stammered to say something to try to right things with Andrea, but before she could find her voice to speak, she realized she was quickly being ushered out of Andrea's office with Andrea exclaiming, "There is *nothing* left for *us* to talk about!" When Colette asked if their children could play together later on in the week, as they commonly did, Andrea replied, "No, that won't be possible anymore!"

Colette was devastated! It was apparent that not only was her four-year friendship with Andrea over, but their children's friendships were also suddenly terminated. How could this be? From the tone of Andrea's voice, Colette assumed that it was something *she* had said or done that was responsible for the ending. As Colette was asked questions in therapy, she realized that she had been observing a pattern in Andrea's behavior during her four years helping in the church office.

As numerous women volunteered countless hours on a weekly basis for Andrea, there was an unstated assumption. Whatever *Andrea* deemed important, everyone in the office needed to make her top priority. Andrea showed no regard for *others'* needs or time constraints. If someone needed to set a personal boundary because her children, her spouse, or her own job or business needed her time and attention (after all, they were volunteers), the woman was subtly shunned by Andrea. There were no rages or outbursts, which an overt narcissist might display. Instead, there was an air of disappointment and the feeling that the person somehow lacked loyalty and had *her* priorities wrong. Then, suddenly, the person was *gone!* There were no discussions about what took place. Some of these women had tried to tell Colette what happened: how they set a boundary and were now shunned by Andrea. Colette couldn't quite make sense of these incidents and assumed that Andrea must have had her reasons.

It became apparent to all of the women in the office that they better not ever disappoint Andrea or they, too, would be devalued and abandoned by Andrea, and they, too, would be kicked out of her presence. Because of this anxiety in the office atmosphere, some women tried to overly please Andrea. Colette noticed that Andrea would then tend to find fault with these women and would criticize them, and even jokingly devalue them in front of the other women. Looking back, it became clearer to Colette that Andrea talked about others in overly idealized or in devalued terms—they either walked on water and had no faults, or, quite simply, there was nothing good about them and they couldn't do anything right!

As is common when people are interacting with a narcissist (even when they don't know that they are), no one ever dared to disagree with Andrea or to give her any negative feedback about herself or her ideas or plans. This, of course, further inflated her own idea that she was always right.

Colette came to realize that when Andrea felt slighted by someone, she "completely vaporized" that person—Andrea devalued her to the point that she no longer existed. She never mentioned that person again, and if the person's name was brought up, Andrea coolly disregarded what was said and acted as if she had never known her. She either changed the subject or made a subtle, devaluing remark such as, "Yes, she's taking time off to 'get herself together!'"

Colette knew that her own time had come. When she was in the same room as Andrea, her presence was never acknowledged: there was no eye contact or "Hello, how are the kids?"

Dr. Stephen Johnson talks about this aspect of narcissism when he says, "As with any person who idealizes, he [the narcissist] is prone to disillusionment when the idealized others fail to live up to his unrealistic expectations...the narcissist sees others not as they are, but as he needs them to be.... People are split into categories, good and bad; they are used but not related to for the people they are. Others are seen not for the gifts they have to share, the limitations they face, and the pain they experience. They are related to only in relation to the narcissist's needs.... We are objects to him, and to the extent that we are narcissistic, others are objects to us. He doesn't really see and hear and feel who we are and, to the extent that we are narcissistic, we do not really see and hear and feel the true presence of others. They, we are objects" (1994, pp.164-165).

CHAPTER 2

GROWING UP IN A NARCISSISTIC FAMILY

In the narcissistic family, children are objects to be used for the selfish needs of the parent (or parents). The children are expected to excel in various talents or athletics, not for their own enjoyment, but to make the parent look good. And to top it all off, kids are supposed to know things without being taught. The parent doesn't spend time teaching the child about things that are new and that the child couldn't possibly have inherent knowledge of. There is no understanding that children go through developmental stages and need help to grow into healthy adults. However, when the child makes a mistake because he didn't inherently know how to act or how to handle a given situation, the parent is shocked and dismayed, and can't begin to understand how or why the child or teen could have blown it like he did. The child is called a stupid idiot—either with words or with a devaluing look. The child internalizes the shame and wonders, "How could I have not known that?" He then vows to himself to try to never be found inadequate again.

Another common characteristic in narcissistic parents is that absolutely nothing is their fault and they apologize for nothing. Because of the parents' perpetual self-righteous stance, children from these families often grow up truly confused. Mom and Dad look so perfect. This leads to feelings like, "I should be so happy. What is wrong with me? I have the perfect family. Maybe it's me. Maybe I'm too selfish or too needy...."

Kate

I (Lisa) first met Kate at my Meier Clinics office when she was in graduate school studying to become a therapist. She was a tall, slender, naturally attractive woman in her early fifties. It became immediately obvious to me that the person who sat in front of me was very different from the person she described herself to be. Kate expressed herself well—in an articulate and insightful way—yet described herself as being way too needy and emotionally dramatic. But she was not coming across this way at all! She said she was unable to maintain healthy relationships because she always "drove people away with her excessive neediness." She said she came from a "great family" and wasn't sure why she had so many problems. She guessed that she might have a genetic disorder like bipolar, or that she may even possibly have a borderline personality disorder (I could tell she was in graduate school learning about various disorders).

As I asked her questions, she shared that her father had been an idealized pastor in a small town. Her mother worked at home and opened up her home several times per week for women's Bible studies. She described her childhood house as always being immaculate and had memories of fresh apple pie baking in the oven. Her mother sewed her and her sister's clothes and her family was the "envy" of the town, she said. She viewed her family as perfect. When she came into therapy, she did not express a single negative feeling regarding her upbringing. Instead, her complaints were always about herself. She would say things like, "There's always been something wrong with me. I always need more than people can give, and that tends to push them away."

Well, as I asked Kate questions, what became increasingly clear to me (and took her a long time to see, because she was so used to blaming herself for everything) was that what was missing from Kate's family when she was growing up was feelings. As she was growing up, when she expressed her thoughts, feelings, and wishes (which often included feelings that she needed more of her mother's attention), her mother would respond in confident tones telling Kate that she was an overly needy, dramatic child and that her feelings and wishes were exaggerated and unrealistic. Furthermore, Kate got the strong impression that she always said the wrong thing at the wrong time—and she came to feel that there was an ugliness or badness inside of her because her mother always looked shocked, overwhelmed, or put out when she learned of any of Kate's thoughts, feelings, or wishes that were different from her own.

Kate assumed her mother's view of her must be true because her mom said things so confidently, and, after all, her "perfect" family was the envy of the town. In addition, Kate's older sister was passive and compliant and tried to make life easier for Mom. This further reinforced Kate's own doubts about herself. She would ask herself, "What is wrong with me? Why do I feel so empty? Why am I so lonely? Mom must be right. I am too needy. My emotions are too intense and dramatic." She began to label her feelings as disgusting and did everything she could to suppress them.

Kate even had to suppress her own strengths around her mother. Her sister had developed a life-threatening eating disorder (which isn't surprising, because she had to suppress all of her feelings, too, and both parents gave the girls the message that fat people are less valuable than thin people). Well, Kate was built with a naturally tall, slender frame, was more outgoing than her older sister, and tended to make friends much more easily. Academics also came easily to Kate. But anytime Kate attempted to share a sense of accomplishment with her mother, she was hushed and told not to talk about it because it would make her sister feel bad and would make her eating disorder worse—so Kate learned to chronically suppress her strengths as well as her feelings.

In contrast to memories of her mother, Kate's memories of her father were more positive. She felt special to him, and he conveyed to her with his eyes and his smile that he was proud of how spunky she was. Unfortunately, her sister's memories of Dad were that he was cold, disapproving, and aloof. Their charming father insisted to his family that they needed to look great in public all the time and he appeared to be ashamed of Kate's sister, who was immensely tall for her age, quite overweight (before the anorexia), and quite shy in public.

When she was a young teen, Kate's family had to abruptly move, because her father was discovered to be having an affair with a woman in the church. This was never discussed or processed in the family, and Kate knew she couldn't express her feelings of loss about moving. Her mother became a bitter, resentful woman, but feelings still weren't expressed or acknowledged. Then, suddenly, when Kate was sixteen, her father dropped dead of a heart attack. She was devastated! She adored her father (more feelings she wasn't allowed to express to her mother). Kate remembered never seeing her mother cry—not even at the funeral.

When I asked Kate what she did to grieve her father's death, she recounted spending hours in her room crying and lamenting over this tragic loss, but she knew that she needed to "get her emotions together" before she exited her room. When I asked if she and her sister were ever able to express their emotions with one another, she realized that they grew up isolated from each other, so, no, they had never talked about their father's death.

Kate grew up in a narcissistic home. And, for Kate, the death of her father was the death of the only part of herself that felt truly alive. While Kate's father had been gone working most of the time, it warmed her heart to see that her father was proud of her and enjoyed and valued her spunky spirit (the spirit that severely got on her mother's nerves). She felt that her father was her only link to what was real inside of her and that he connected with her real self—the true person she was created to be—before she began suppressing most of herself to please her mother.

The unfortunate reality for Kate was that actually both of her parents were narcissistic. While Kate received affectionate responses from her father, in her sister's interactions with him he was cold, critical, and devaluing, just as Kate's mother acted toward Kate.

This can be a common theme in narcissistic homes. Each parent picks a child to idealize and one to devalue—one can do no right and the other can do no wrong. The parents are sometimes united in their views of who is good and who is bad, but often, they choose different kids to show their favor or disdain. Since narcissists deny their own faults, they reject the child who is most likely to remind them of those faults. In most narcissistic families, the dad will be harshest with his oldest son and the mom with her oldest daughter, because that is usually the child who the narcissistic parent can dump his or her own badness into as a scapegoat. This is called projection. Most parents do this unconsciously to some extent, but narcissistic parents do so in a more dramatic, excessive fashion.

This tendency leads to further jealousy in the family dynamics, because the spouse and other children watch one child receive an inordinate amount of attention and praise from one parent while the rest of the family literally feels unseen, and their own good is unrecognized by this parent.

In one of Kate's sessions, a rather disturbing memory of her father came back to her. After Kate's mom had spent years maintaining a perfect home for numerous weekly church women's events, as well as being the seamstress who made all of the costumes for each of the church's productions, she began having some health problems and needed a cane to help her walk. Kate's disturbing recollection was that her parents were invited out, and she heard her father exclaim to her mother, "I can't be seen out in public with a cripple!" That is narcissism. Shortly thereafter, her father began having his affair.

This is a common theme in the narcissistic home. It is everyone's job to make the family have an ideal image in public. How a child is really doing is not of concern in the family, nor is who he or she really is. And this is the silent pain, the true loneliness and despair felt in the hearts of anyone in the family who can still feel. Because people in the community often experience the narcissist as outgoing, warm, and relational, they often envy his spouse and children and think, "They are so lucky to have him." But what no one knows is that this man who shows grace, empathy, and good social skills in public does not bring these characteristics home with him at night. At home, because of his fears of intimacy, he is usually distant and aloof, and he tends to be moody. He does not ask his family members how they are doing. He does not pick up on the emotional temperature of the home. He is not tuned into the fact that no one is talking or interacting when he is around. There is no talk of emotions in this home, no talk of feelings, no sharing of struggles or pain.

As we just observed in Kate's case, displays of emotion from a spouse or a child are often labeled as dramatic and are often criticized and devalued. Children are often given messages like "You have always had such an excessive need for attention," because children are truly in need of a lot of attention, and these needs get in the way of the parent's agenda. Children often feel that they are in the way and are not to interrupt or bother the parent from things that are truly important. The needs of the parent are put in front of the children's needs again and again. These children often begin to have the same symptoms of children of alcoholics, wherein the children revolve their lives and all of their own energy and attention around the parent's mood, needs, etc., and the children's needs are truly neglected over and over. The children are robbed of childhood.

However, a child or teen can receive an inordinate amount of attention from the narcissistic parent if he or she is doing something of star quality that receives attention from the community, such as if he is the high school football team's great quarterback or if she is running for Little Miss in the local beauty pageant. This is because the child is a narcissistic extension of the parent's self—the parent and the child are not viewed as two separate people in the mind of a narcissist. Hence, the parent takes full credit for the child or teen's success. But this is also true regarding any failures, so this narcissistic parent is often the obnoxious parent at sports games who is raging at the referee. (Don't worry. Non-narcissistic people do this too when adrenaline gets too high, as it is prone to do at sporting events!) Rather than allow the child to excel in his or her own natural bent, abilities, or interests, the parent often pushes the child to excel in whatever the narcissistic parent felt deficient in. The child's duty is to excel in areas that compensate for the perceived weakness of the parent. Even if the parent is very successful in a talent or sport, the child may be pushed to go into that same sport or talent.

What is different with the narcissistic parent is that he incessantly brags about his star child. In fact, it is often hard to get a word in otherwise. No matter what subject is brought up, he will find a way to immediately bring the conversation back to prattling on and on about his child's latest performance, success, etc. Other parents will be rooting for the whole team, but not this parent. He views others on his son or daughter's team as major competition, and whenever another team member does exceptionally well, he is scheming about how to help his child become even better!

In cases where a child is actually helping to prop up the narcissistic family's image, the parent(s) will protect this child at all costs. If another parent, a coach, or a teacher gives feedback that the child has been unkind or is not performing well, the narcissistic parent is likely to attack the source giving the unpleasant information rather than look into a potential problem with the star child.

In many narcissistic families, the child is often devalued or harshly criticized for "making the family look bad" when negative feedback occurs. The child or teen is then commanded to "Get it together!" And yet, no teaching or support is offered by the parents to help make things better. Again, in these families, children are just supposed to know how to grow and develop into healthy, functioning adults without being taught. This, of course, breeds a lot of performance anxiety as these children try to guess at all of the environmental clues of how to do things right. What contributes to even more anxiety is the fact that positive attention and recognition for having value as a person only come during times of major success.

While this person is growing more of a performance-based self (false self), the real person, who was created to be unique and different from anyone else, is getting lost (suppressed from conscious awareness)—like you see in Kate's case. She hid her emotions to protect herself from being constantly labeled as dramatic. As time went on she felt her emotions less and less as she internalized her mother's voice more and more. Now, in her own voice, she told herself that she was too needy and emotionally dramatic and she feared that if she allowed herself to be who she was created to be (her real self), her emotional neediness would push people away.

Unfortunately, when we are emotionally numb, we're likely to hang out with people who are emotionally insensitive, because this helps to keep our hearts in hiding. Our hearts are not tempted to come out of their emotional prisons unless they are invited out by people who offer warmth and support. This, of course, often leads the adult child of the narcissistic family to marry someone who is fairly narcissistic. We will see later how this happened with Kate. Another outcome of growing up in a narcissistic home is that sometimes the adult child internalizes the narcissism and then struggles with narcissism him or herself, as we'll see in the following chapter.

CHAPTER 3

THE CREATION OF NARCISSISM

Two major camps of thought exist regarding what creates narcissism or narcissistic defense mechanisms in a child. One is that a child is over-idealized to meet the emotional needs of the parent and thus develops feelings of superiority and entitlement from being overindulged. The second camp suggests that narcissism is basically a defense mechanism that is a reaction to hurt or trauma to a child's sense of self. The emotional insult occurs in the relationship with a major attachment figure—most often the mother or father. In our offices, we have heard the deepest, innermost secrets, thoughts, and feelings of thousands of clients studying their childhoods as well as their current conflicts, which are often related. So from our experience, we believe that both camps of thought about the origins of narcissism offer information that will benefit you.

The first idea suggests that as a child, the narcissistic person was overindulged, idealized, and not held responsible for her actions. Specifically, this school of thought implies extreme behavior wherein the "…parents come to view their child as 'God's gift to mankind.' These parents pamper and indulge their youngsters in ways that teach them that their every wish is a command, that they can receive without giving in return, and that they deserve prominence without even minimal effort.... In short order, children with such experiences will learn to view themselves as special beings, and learn to expect subservience from others; they begin to recognize that their mere existence is sufficient to provide pleasure to others and that their every action evokes commendation and praise. Unfortunately, they fail to learn how to cooperate and share or to think of the desires and interests of others. They acquire little sense of inter-personal responsibility and few skills for the give-and-take of social life. The family world revolves around them.... Such youngsters learn not only to take others for granted and to exploit them for personal benefit, but they also learn to see others as weak and subservient. By their fawning and self-demeaning behaviors, the parents of future narcissists have provided them with an image of others as manipulable, docile, and yielding. This view not only enhances the narcissists' image of their own specialness but serves to strengthen their inclination to exploit others. Seeing others as weak and submissive allows them to ride roughshod over their interests with impunity" (Millon, 1996, pp. 419-421).

It is normal that when we have a child, we realize that our child is truly a gift to us. Of course, we all want our children to realize their own unique specialness, but we want our children to have realistic views of themselves. We also want them to develop responsible consciences and to learn to love and be loved as well as to give and to receive.

Parents who completely spoil their child do not do this because they love their child so much. Parents who love their child discipline their child, facing temporary rejection, for the good of the child—preparing the child to succeed, to love, and to be loved in a world that does have boundaries. Narcissistic parents are often the ones who love themselves too much to face the rejection of their child (because children hate being told, "no"), therefore, they spoil her to avoid confrontation or rejection. But sometimes parents with low self-esteem also fear the rejection of their child. Sometimes these parents even have a hard time saying "no" when their child grows up to be a thirty-year-old freeloader, living with them or supported by them, often using their money for illegal drugs or other addictions..

Children need to be loved and taught that they are each uniquely special. But if young children's natural narcissistic tendencies go unchecked by reasonable boundaries, they will have an unreasonable amount of narcissistic tendencies.

It's amazing to me (Paul) that all of these findings from modern psychiatric research only reiterate the personal findings of brilliant King Solomon 3000 years ago, who taught in his book of Proverbs that a child left to totally rule himself will end up bringing his mother to shame. He also taught that parents who love their young child will discipline their child diligently (not harshly, but consistently), and that if they deprive the child of discipline, they will spoil that child.

Anthony

Anthony was raised with a silver spoon in his mouth. Born to multimillionaire parents, he was idealized from the time he was an infant. He was catered to and was given no consequences for the massive tantrums he threw anytime there was a threat that he might not get his way. His parents avoided his rejection, so his tantrums resulted in his being given what he wanted—which reinforced his haughty behavior. He became more and more arrogant, which was a quality actually admired in his family.

Remember Kate? After years of alcohol abuse, she got into recovery, and then she met the man that she thought would redeem her—Anthony! In the beginning, Kate wasn't sure she liked Anthony very much, but, as usual, she assumed she couldn't trust her own emotions. Her mother raved about Anthony and was so happy that she could finally brag to her friends about Kate's life; up until then, Kate's life had been in shambles.

Now that Kate was in recovery, she started her own business, and it was quite successfully taking off. She was beginning to feel a sense of accomplishment and felt she was finally beginning to get in touch with herself as a person with gifts and talents that she was born with. Her narcissistic mother gave her no acknowledgement for her creativity and solid business sense, but instead told her she'd be a fool if she messed things up with Anthony. Being accustomed to her mother's narcissistic manipulation while growing up trained Kate to be more susceptible to—even codependently addicted to—the manipulations of Anthony, rendering her relatively blind to these manipulations until well into the relationship.

Most humans probably have a tendency to fall in love—a transference phenomenon usually, rather than true love—with people similar to the parent of the opposite sex or to the most abusive parent of either sex. I (Paul) once treated a famous, rich, and beautiful movie star in her thirties who had already divorced seven physically abusive narcissists, thinking each was a good guy when she married him. Her codependent addiction to narcissists came from having a totally narcissistic, physically and sexually abusive father and getting used to seeing herself and men in general within that context. It was as though she had invisible antennas coming out of her brain that went zap whenever she met a good-looking, narcissistic man like her father. Fortunately, she gained insight and developed boundaries and never made that mistake again.

Meanwhile—back to Kate's story—Anthony would fly into town to see Kate and would take her on intriguing trips. She eventually decided to close her business and to marry this man because "he was somebody." When she was around Anthony, she figured that he made her somebody too. When Kate had broken up with Anthony for a short period while dating, she went back to feeling like a nobody—like she was nothing without him. In our current American culture, how often do we hear ridiculous popular songs that whine out the message, "I just can't live without you," or "I'm nothing, Baby, without you"? We (the authors) prefer songs that tell the truth, like Tina Turner's accurate song about codependency that informs us, "What's love got to do, got to do with it? What's love but a secondhand emotion?" The kind of fake love Tina was singing about is a secondhand transference phenomenon, like my (Paul's) movie star patient marrying men like her dad because of her addictive need to fix him or fill the lonely void his lack of genuine love left in her soul.

We can see that this is what happened with Kate. During the time of her breakup with Anthony, Kate's mother kept trying to persuade Kate to win Anthony back rather than looking at the pain the relationship had been creating in her daughter's life and listening to her daughter's sense that something didn't seem right. Kate's mom, being a narcissist, wasn't concerned about her daughter's well-being. Instead, she was focused upon how her daughter's success and money could make her (the mom) feel important and could give her more bragging rights with her peers. Thus, Kate's mother reinforced Kate's deepest insecurity: "You'll be nothing without him." Kate knew that her mother deeply believed that only wealth, status, sex appeal, or a position of power could possibly give a person value. In fact, Kate's mother directly told her, "That's why I married your father—because he was somebody, a pastor everyone looked up to—and then I set out to become the best pastor's wife I could be."

In reality, what we have observed in thousands of people over the years is that people who are only focused upon sex, power, and money—which we refer to as fool's gold rather than true gold—end up living empty, unfulfilling lives. When people are able to love and receive love from people who accept them for who they really are, we see true lifelong happiness and contentment.

Unfortunately, shortly into her marriage to Anthony, Kate realized that not all would be bliss. She came to realize that Anthony was severely addicted to hash (a drug similar to marijuana, but much more potent). She became the cook and housekeeper while he partied with his friends. Because of Kate's age, she wanted to begin a family and was soon blessed with a son and a daughter. Kate had hoped that having a family would settle Anthony down and perhaps he would become more family-oriented. Instead, she began to feel more and more like a nanny. Anthony acted okay toward her as long as she asked him for nothing and as long as she brought the children to occasions where he wanted to show them off; she understood that she was responsible for keeping them from disrupting his party life in any way.

Kate was grateful that she was given children later in life and loved being a mom, so she would have likely stayed in this empty marriage forever, except Anthony then had an affair, quickly divorced Kate, and wanted his new girlfriend to become Mom to his and Kate's four- and six-year-old kids! Kate was literally discarded—as if she didn't exist (talk about being treated as an object that is not seen or heard or felt).

As stated at the beginning of the chapter, the other camp of thought regarding the causes of narcissism emphasizes that narcissism is not always simply the result of being spoiled in childhood. The second camp suggests that narcissism is basically a defense mechanism that is a reaction to hurt or trauma to a person's sense of self. The emotional insult occurs in the relationship with a major attachment figure—most often the mother or father. When parents have unrealistic views regarding the needs of their infants and young children and react to their children with unhealthy emotional responses, these children then need to build thoughts that help protect them from becoming too emotionally overwhelmed.

When a mother is responsive to her infant's voice and mimics him, he is delighted that he was able to produce this response in her. This will encourage him to engage with her more and more. He will come to feel very significant to his mother as he senses that his mere presence brings her joy. As she meets not only his physical needs, but his needs for emotional connection, his anxiety about his helpless state will be soothed. This is how healthy emotional attachments are formed. As time goes on, this is also how a healthy sense of self is formed—a belief of being significant and loved.

However, in contrast, if an infant's needs are neglected, or even if he has all of his physical needs taken care of but his mother does not make eye contact when she is not feeding him or changing him, he will begin to feel emotional pain because he is lonely. He will make cooing sounds and will long for her gaze. When he cannot get the reaction he needs from her, he will begin feeling a sense of despair. As time goes on, he will not build a healthy sense of self, because he will not internalize the belief that he is significant and loved. It is overwhelming for a young child to fathom the thought of not being significant or loved, so he will begin building some alternate scenarios in his head. He will surmise that he doesn't really need that emotional connection. He will learn to devalue love and the emotional needs and feelings in himself and in others.

As a child's desire to love and be loved is rejected, she has to compensate in order to live in a loveless world. Some children grow up and overcome these losses to become some of the nicest human beings we know. Others grow up to become narcissists, learning that manipulating their loveless environment is the only way they know to survive.

When children or teens from narcissistic homes tend to inflate their own sense of self-worth, it is because they have assumed the stance that to be human is to be weak and have vowed that they will never again allow themselves to be in vulnerable positions where they could be exposed as weak, because that would make them worthless. This is because, in narcissistic families, kids are supposed to just know how to develop into functioning adults. They are not taught skills, nor are their developmental stages taken into consideration. This, of course, breeds a lot of performance anxiety in the children as they try to guess at all of the environmental cues of how to do things right. They are shamed and humiliated at times when they simply don't know something. Therefore, they begin to disown their own vulnerability and truly believe that they are not allowed to ever not know something.

While these people are growing more of a performance-based self (false self), they come to believe that they will only be deemed worthy if they are great. They have to inflate how worthy they believe they are because they have learned that people are either idealized or devalued, and they must protect themselves from the pain they have experienced at times when their human vulnerability was attacked and shamed. They never want to feel utterly weak and humiliated again. They need to believe that they are invincible, that no one can get them anymore. They come to believe that people are dangerous and only love them when they're great. Therefore, they begin to devalue love and devalue those who are able to express genuine love to them.

Because their vulnerable, loving, needing hearts were devalued as children, they will come to have contempt for their own feelings of love and vulnerability that sneak into their consciousness from time to time, and they will tend to attack any vulnerable characteristics that others show. Whatever was devalued in them, they now devalue in others. It is all they know to do. They don't know that their parents were wrong. They don't know that their parents devalued the best part of them—their hearts! They don't know that what healthy people want is to be able to share their own strengths and weaknesses with others who will appreciate and value them for who they really are. People with narcissistic defenses don't know that their daily decisions are based primarily on lies they learned in childhood, and this is why they continually wonder why their decisions do not bring them the love, joy, and meaning that they truly need.

Narcissists don't realize that their puffed up self-righteousness is actually distancing, is viewed as obnoxious, and makes them look insecure to healthier people. They don't know this because in their families, their parents admitted no fault and apologized for nothing. This led them to believe that people aren't supposed to make mistakes.

In fact, narcissistic parents have a remarkable ability of turning things around in a nanosecond, and they blame their children for their own actions. These parents did what they did because the children "pushed them to do it!" The children internalize tremendous anxiety and self-doubt because of all of the blame projected onto them. They vow to try to suppress whatever part of themselves that they believe caused the parents' reaction. For example, if the children expressed anger to their parents because they believed a situation was unfair (as kids often do) and, in return, they were verbally attacked and shamed, the children will slowly kill off their own feelings so that as time goes by, they no longer possess much awareness of their own feelings, wants, or needs, or what they believe to be fair or unfair. Furthermore, they kill (unconsciously suppress) their own fears, insecurities, and weaknesses. To go on living, they have to build their own protective worlds in their minds—worlds where they are adequate, even superior—so as to never be exposed as weak or bad again.

Claudia

Claudia, the adult child of a narcissistic mother, remembers emotionally collapsing and losing her sense of self when she was fifteen. She says, "After lying on my bed, sobbing my guts out, I remember declaring to my mother inside my own head, 'Okay, you win!' I became totally compliant. All of my thoughts would now be centered only upon her. I began to think her thoughts, I began to look and act like her, I began to like only what she liked, I began to hate what she hated. After being devalued my whole life for my feelings or opinions, I couldn't take it anymore. I didn't have the strength to keep fighting her."

Claudia continued, saying, "I made a vow that I would never again give her the opportunity to label me as emotionally dramatic. I became quiet and reserved and inflated in my own opinion of myself. Looking perfect became of utmost importance. No longer could I ever be seen as having any flaws. I put a smile on my face to always project that I had it all together. I could no longer feel the pain of having insecurities or weaknesses, or fear. I was above all of that now. I became truly comfortably numb in my grandiosity. I was no longer vulnerable. What a relief! Never again would I express vulnerable emotions to have them mocked and devalued. Never again would I express a need, only to have it met with disdain or contempt. Human vulnerability became my enemy. Emotional closeness became my biggest threat because then, I might feel my heart again. No! Instead, I sought relationships wherein I was looked up to and idealized. This kept me at the safe distance I was seeking, because there is no vulnerability or true intimacy when someone is beneath us. It is only dangerous if we love them as an equal, because this is when our hearts become vulnerable."

Claudia went on to say, "What amazed me was that the more grandiose I became in my own head, the more my mother revered me. She no longer put me down. She now idealized me! I literally began believing that I truly was more special, unique, and more knowledgeable than others. If anyone questioned me or hinted that I may not be right about something, I became shocked, incredulous! I would attempt to enlighten him, and if I were unsuccessful, I would disregard him as a person who just didn't get it! I was shocked and saddened the day my therapist pointed out to me that I was treating the people closest to me the way my mother had treated me. She said I was giving them the experience of what it was like to be me growing up. I vowed then to begin making some serious changes in my life."

Dr. Stephen Johnson encompasses both views of the origin of narcissism— either that it's the result of being spoiled in childhood or it occurs as a defensive reaction to abuse or neglect—in his statements regarding causal factors of narcissism. He states, "The reconstruction of narcissistic cases often yields the fact that the individual was repeatedly put down or 'narcissistically injured' in the expression of his ambitious self-expression, or he was idealized, and therefore expected to provide far more gratification, excitement, or meaning for his parents than was possible, or both. It is not uncommon in the reconstruction of these cases that one parent was more idealizing, and that the narcissistic injury initiated by that parent came from the child's inability to live up to the inflated expectations. Simultaneously, the other parent can be threatened by the child's real magnificence and the spouse's extravagant attention to the child. Unable to deal with all of that, the other parent may humiliate and shame the child, narcissistically injuring him more directly" (p. 41).

Johnson goes on to say, "Narcissistic injury can take an infinite number of specific forms, but essentially it occurs when the environment needs the individual to be something substantially different from what he or she really is. Essentially, the message to the emerging person is, 'Don't be who you are, be who I need you to be. Who you are disappoints me, threatens me, angers me, and over stimulates me. Be what I want and I will love you'" (pp.155-156). This is, of course, the ultimate conditional love, which is not love at all. Conditional love means that if you pretend you are who I want you to be, I will pretend to love you. I may even fool both you and myself that I really do.

Things to Keep in Mind Before Reading the Narcissism Questionnaire:

Now, before you panic, we want to make it very clear that many children and most teenagers will tend to look narcissistic some or even most of the time. That is normal for their ages and developmental stages. I (Paul) learned in my psychiatry residency at Duke Medical Center that any normal thirteen-year-old would be considered crazy and narcissistic if an adult. I had the privilege of rearing six teenagers, all of whom went through an early teen stage of thinking they knew everything and I knew nothing! So keep this in mind. The following questionnaire applies to adults—not teens.

Furthermore, we want you to keep in mind that where narcissism gets tricky is when the more severely narcissistically defended someone is, the less they will be able to admit these deeper feelings of inadequacy. If we have people in our lives who read this book and tell us that they have consistently seen narcissistic behavior in us, we need to keep reading about narcissism and see if more unconscious feelings and memories get evoked. We need to realize that non-narcissistic people won't hate our human weaknesses and vulnerabilities. These are the things that endear us to them. When we are real and vulnerable with them, they feel they are able to connect with our hearts. What stresses them out and drives them crazy about us are our attempts to constantly push them away, our refusal to accept responsibility for our mistakes, and our stubborn and prideful stance toward them. They love us because every once in a while, we show them our true hearts and our vulnerabilities. It is then that they can temporarily feel our love for them and can see that we are truly suffering within our own hearts and minds. This is why they have stayed. They have tried to be patient, but often they are growing weary. It will change our lives for the better when we move toward becoming more real with ourselves and with our relationships with the people closest to us. It will dramatically improve the quality of our happiness and personal satisfaction as we all seek to uncover any narcissistic traits we may have.

Narcissism Questionnaire

The following are questions we can ask ourselves (and others) in order to check for accidental, unconscious narcissistic traits, so we can become more loving and experience more love, joy, and meaning in our lives by operating on truth rather than lies we may have been taught by our parents or others in our childhood (or by others in our adulthood):

1. Do I have a humble heart? Do I realize I'm not perfect and have both strengths as well as weaknesses—and don't feel overly threatened to acknowledge either of them?

2. Do I have empathy for others? Can I put myself in their shoes and imagine how my behavior has impacted them? For

example, do I slow down my driving when passengers say they are frightened?

3. Can I admit when I'm wrong? Can I apologize with a caring heart, and do I seek to make things right to help repair the rift in the relationship? (It takes a humble heart to be able to do this.)

4. Do I think I deserve special favors and preferential treatment and should be treated as having special status? For example, do I ask for things that aren't on the restaurant menu or talk to the server in a haughty tone of voice that makes him feel inferior to me?

5. Do I tend to think in terms that categorize people in my head as superior or inferior to myself, rather than believe we are all equal?

6. Do I tend to talk about others behind their backs in a tone of voice or in a manner that puts them down or makes them seem inferior?

7. Am I able to share my strengths and weaknesses with others, or do I tend to brag about my accomplishments, but hide my weaknesses?

8. Am I shocked or do I become angry when others have an opinion that is different from my own?

9. Do I try to exert extensive control over my family members so they dress or act in certain ways so they don't tarnish my image to others? For example, do I try to get my kids to pursue sports or careers that I want them to do rather than honor what they want?

10. Do I often feel envious of others or believe they are envious of me?

11. Do I take advantage of others or use others to achieve my own ends without enough regard for their feelings or needs?

12. Do I believe I am special or unique and can only be understood by others who also are special or unique?

13. Do I expect others to automatically comply with my wishes, and do I become shocked and outraged when they don't?

14. Do I feel an increase in my self-worth when I associate with others who possess beauty, wealth, high status, or power?

15. Do I tend to need excessive admiration from others, and do I seek this attention from others—even in subtle ways? For example, do I talk to strangers in a restaurant to get their attention?

16. Do I get energized by thoughts of myself possessing more intelligence, attractiveness, wealth, status, or power than others?

17. Do I take pride in being able to do things without the help of others, and do I believe that to need others or need help from others makes a person weak or pathetic?

18. Do I feel safest psychologically when I feel alone?

19. Do I feel threatened psychologically when I feel I am becoming attached to and emotionally dependent upon another person?

20. Do I verbally attack or withdraw from a person who has pointed out my failure, and do I devalue them (put them down) as a way to inflate my own self-worth?

21. When I experience failure (as all people do), do I either become grandiose in my head (wherein I increase my self-worth by believing I never fail), or do I experience strong feelings of self-loathing or self-contempt because of my failure or mistake (self-

devaluation) and feel shame, humiliation, rage, inferiority, or emptiness?

Narcissistic Traits Versus Narcissistic Personality Disorder

We believe it is helpful to look at personality characteristics on a continuum. We all exhibit various traits, coping mechanisms, behaviors, relational patterns, and so on. Some of them work for us; some of them don't. Some of them improve our lives and our relationships; some of them hurt ourselves or the ones we love. And all of us have at least a few narcissistic personality tendencies. Even Mother Theresa humbly admitted her own need for prayer and forgiveness!

Healthy people continually self-evaluate and try to learn and grow. They accept feedback from others and understand that they may not always be right in how they view themselves or situations. When it comes to their attention that a certain attitude or behavior is getting in the way of their relationships, goals, or aspirations, they attempt to make changes to improve the quality of their lives.

It should be noted that it often takes quite a bit of time, consideration, and focus for adults to begin exhibiting new behaviors. Often this is just because old habits can be hard to break. However, the more a person is character disordered (again, it is always on a continuum), the more his thoughts, attitudes, feelings, and behaviors (traits) interfere with his ability to maintain healthy relationships with others. The intensity of his character disorder is defined by his level of insight (whether he is able to view himself realistically—even after receiving feedback from others), his ability to have empathy for how his behaviors make another person feel, and the degree of motivation he shows to change his behavior because of the insights he lacks in viewing himself and others in a realistic way.

Therefore, a person is character disordered when:

You Might Be A Narcissist if...

1. He lacks realistic insight into himself.

2. He tends to project blame onto others (accuses them of doing the things that he is actually doing rather than taking responsibility for his actions).

3. He has little or no care about how his behavior hurts the people he loves.

4. He shows little or no motivation to change.

Be encouraged that if you have read this much of this book and not only desire to learn better ways to interact with narcissists, but also want to become less narcissistic and more loving yourself, then, even if you have twenty-one out of twenty-one narcissistic tendencies, you are on stepping-stones that will lead you down a path of truth that will enhance the quality of your life and the lives of those you love (or are learning to love).

In order to address our own narcissism, we need to find safe people with whom we can begin to explore the truth of who we really are. We need to receive empathy from them for our insecurities. We need to gain insight and empathy for our own emotional injuries that were created from the experiences we had wherein our needs, our feelings, or our imperfections were shamed. By receiving empathy we gain the capacity to give empathy to others.

CHAPTER 4

THE STRUGGLES OF THE ADULT CHILD OF A NARCISSISTIC FAMILY

My (Cynthia's) parents were beautiful-looking people. In fact, a family member once told me that my mom took great pride in her own beauty and in the fact that she married such a handsome man—and knew they would have beautiful children. However, I, their first child, was born cross-eyed and far-sighted and had to wear thick corrective glasses. I was told that my mom was devastated, and that it "broke her heart to see your defect." I was also told "her dream was shattered!"

As a young, gregarious child, I learned that I could get my dad's attention by making him laugh—which he rarely did in the stoic environment of our home. He gave me attention if I danced, performed tricks, and told funny stories. The other way I could relate with him was to listen to his unending tales of his experiences through the world (with often feigned attention as I grew older, because I got really bored listening to him repeat the same stories over and over). This gave him the constant attention he craved. He acted as if he were on stage and would go on and on with his monologues, expecting our family to remain completely engaged. Never did he ask us questions about our thoughts, our experiences, and ourselves. He really didn't know us and didn't seem to even see us—not for whom we were. We seemed to only exist when we were making him feel good about himself.

I learned that any attention I would ever receive from my mom and dad would be by cajoling them, entertaining them, or, on occasion, pitching an emotional fit that would arrest their attention for a time. This last ploy felt worth it all if, for one precious half an hour, I could (I believed) commune with my dad's heart. In these rare moments, it felt as though all of heaven's eyes were on me as my dad actually listened to my heart. Just having him finally hear me made my problems (which were mostly the haunted, terrifying feelings of being absolutely alone and abandoned in this world) feel like they were dissipating. Unfortunately, his attention was short-lived, and he would return back into his own disconnected world when things calmed down. Any further expressions of emotions were met, as usual, from both Mom and Dad, with a raised eyebrow, a devaluing look, and chastising words of how I was born to be an "unusually dramatic child."

As I heard this drama queen message throughout the years, I came to truly believe that I must have, in fact, been born feeling way too many emotions and that my desire to get emotionally close to people would only repulse them. In reality, I did have too much emotion for my narcissistic parents, but I learned, later in life, that healthier people weren't repulsed by my heart, my feelings, or me. They actually told me that it was my heart and my ability to express my feelings that attracted them the most to me! While this initially shocked and confused me, as time (and therapy) went on, I was able to become in touch with and learn to enjoy the real me I was created to be.

The False Self

Because adult children of narcissists were not allowed to express how they really felt or who they really were as children, by adulthood they have learned to become perpetual actors. As adults, they put smiles on their faces and are able to convince others, and even themselves, that they are quite fine. In reality, most of the time, they're actually very unaware of how they're really feeling or doing.

When they were children, they received very little instruction from their parents. They learned to watch their parents' moods and to guess at expectations. They were given many messages that they were just supposed to know how to act and how to do things to make their parents proud and the family look good at all times. How they were feeling or really doing was of no consequence.

By adulthood, they have become quite adept at reading people and situations and can fake it through parties, business engagements, church socials, or even dinner parties in their own homes. They seem genuinely fine. Yet, often, as the years go by, they become more and more aware that there is a deep sense of loneliness and emptiness growing within them, because there is little connection inside of themselves with their own hearts—with their real self, the separate individual (separate from who their narcissistic parents needed them to be). Their real self is who God created them to be with their own strengths, inherent weaknesses, talents, unique characteristics, and needs for love and human connectedness.

Remember, when Kate and Cynthia attempted to convey how they were feeling to their narcissistic parents, they were labeled again and again as too sensitive, too needy, or too dramatic. Their feelings were not heard, acknowledged, or connected with, but, instead, were devalued. The honest expressions of their hearts were not met with comfort or warmth. Their hearts felt neither love nor acceptance, but instead felt more and more shame, and, as time went on, they truly came to believe that their real selves—who they were created to be—were not good and were too needy, too dependent, or too defective. Their experiences taught them that feeling and expressing their thoughts, feelings, hopes, and dreams only got them into more trouble and only led to the additional pain of being devalued again and again.

Adult children from narcissistic families often come to lack true confidence in their own feelings and beliefs and believe that their only choice is to live in the false self. As they did in their childhoods, they continue to take cues from external sources about what to think, feel, and believe rather than listen to or trust their own thoughts and feelings. This chapter will shed light on some of the struggles and difficulties that emerge from denying who we really are and attempting to live life as who we think we should be.

Perfectionism

While attempting to live up to the ideal self, individuals from narcissistic homes tend to develop many struggles with perfectionism. As children, their own humanity is shamed. Their parents don't spend time teaching or instructing them in things that are new. There is no understanding in the family that kids go through developmental stages and need help and practice to grow into healthy adults. These children are devalued when they don't know something or when they make a mistake, so they think, "I should have known" and "Why didn't I know how to do that?" To defend against being ridiculed, they work harder and harder at trying to get things right. Additionally, they often have never seen their parents apologize for or even acknowledge their own mistakes, so they come to the conclusion that mistakes aren't to be made.

By adulthood, they have often become consumed with trying to live up to the narcissistic parent's ideals haunting them in their own heads. While growing up, their homes often look like museums or just-cleaned hotel rooms. Usually, these children are not taught how to do chores because their parents do not have the patience to teach them, nor could the parent stand to allow the job to be done imperfectly while the child is still learning. In adulthood, having not learned or practiced how to do chores growing up, they usually feel completely overwhelmed with how much work it takes to make a house and yard look perfect.

Sometimes, perfectionists take on the role of being the critical evaluators of others and become overly focused on others' behaviors while denying their own faults (like Lisa did). Other times, they become overly critical of themselves and will easily think that everything is their own fault and will over-apologize for things they didn't even cause (like Kate did).

Addictons

All Addictions Are Driven by Three Things: Shame, Lack of Connectedness, and Suppressed Emotions

Because of internalized shame, adults from narcissistic families can't allow themselves to feel their own humanity (their weaknesses, fears, and insecurities). They feel terrified to get too close to others because they fear that if others come to truly know them, and discover the truth about them, they will surely expose their weaknesses and reject them.

However, as humans, we were not created to be able to live emotionally disconnected from others. When we attempt to live too independently from others, eventually a sense of loneliness and despair grows deep within us. For years, we try to suppress our feelings and try to deny, even to ourselves, how we really feel about ourselves. As with anyone who suppresses many emotions, adults and teens from narcissistic families become prone to various addictions.

The addiction chosen will depend on a variety of genetic, family, and environmental factors, as well as the choices the child makes growing up. For example, a daughter whose narcissistic mother depends on her to be her best friend will become over-enmeshed with her mother and overly dependent upon her mother's decisions, and will tend to become bulimic (vomit on purpose for weight control) or anorexic. Other male and female children of narcissistic parents become codependent—addicted to future relationships with narcissistic people who will continue to treat them in the ways they have become accustomed to.

Addictions can be to drugs, alcohol, or sex, but they can also be to perfectionism (having a perfect house, a perfect physical appearance, a perfect family), workaholism, codependency (believing it is our job to fix, change, stop, or control others), food, exercise, legalism, gambling, the internet, and hobbies: just about anything that becomes the predominant focus of our lives and is hurting ourselves or the people we love. Addictions don't stop immediately once we gain that insight (and we find that we are unable to decrease our behavior to healthy levels that are not causing damage to ourselves or our relationships with significant others).

The primary function of addictions is that they help us feel emotionally numb because, even when we're not taking a mood-altering substance, the constant drivenness we feel when we're addicted consumes our thoughts and gives our minds an excuse to be constantly busy, and this does not allow us time to stop and feel.

Anna

Anna sought help at the Meier Clinics because she was suicidal. Her affair with a married man had just ended when he chose to stay with his wife and two young children. Anna was devastated. In her therapy, as she explored why she entered a sexual relationship with a married man, it became apparent that she not only struggled with alcoholism, but also with sexual addiction. The rush of adrenaline she experienced while attempting to entice an unavailable man into an illicit affair helped distract her from the immense emptiness and chronic loneliness etched into her heart from growing up with two narcissistic parents.

The only way Anna was able to gain attention from her parents as a young child was when her mom dressed her up like a beautiful porcelain doll. Her mom would show her off to her father, who was always emotionally distant. This would cause him to actually put down his paper momentarily, and he would get a sparkle in his eye and would comment on her beauty. It was always short-lived, but she learned to take what she could get. Now she was repeating her childhood by seducing (or yielding to the seductions of) a father substitute. As therapists, we have seen this scenario a thousand times.

Anna's family was involved in politics, so she got an advanced degree in political science. However, after she attained all of her school goals, her sense of direction waned and her sense of emptiness, loneliness, and disconnection became more than she could bear. She started drinking and discovered that seducing men temporarily assuaged her deep feelings of inadequacy. A father-like narcissist's focused attention and admiration temporarily made her feel loved, valued, and worthy. For a short time, she didn't feel the piercing loneliness inside of her that made her want to die. The attention of a man falsely and temporarily filled the hole in her soul left by her parents. It fulfilled her unconscious desire to fix her childhood by fixing this new father substitute. Make sense yet? Relationships are never as simple as they seem.

When Anna began attending Alcoholics Anonymous, she experienced the compassion for her true self, understanding for her failures, and empathy for her broken heart that she had always longed for. In response to her recovery group's assignment to make a list of major resentments, Anna wrote, "I resent my mom for not being interested in the real ME, for treating me like HER appendage, and for trying to turn me into her 'IDEAL'—whatever that was or is. And I resent my father for being so narcissistic that he only gave me attention when I looked BEAUTIFUL."

During her therapy, Anna was able to grieve the losses she experienced in childhood as well as relationship losses she experienced as an adult. She learned that suppressing her feelings only depleted the serotonin in her brain, which caused clinical depression, driving her to drink more to numb her pain. And, learning that excessive alcohol also caused serotonin depletion, which drove her deeper into depression, helped reinforce her decision to no longer abuse alcohol. Additionally, she learned that her sex addiction with unavailable men only replayed her childhood trauma. She learned that in order to recover from her narcissist addiction, she needed to seek equal relationships with people with whom she could be her real self. By healing those wounds from the past, when she was thirty-nine she ended up falling in love with and marrying a healthy, loving, caring man.

Passivity

Adults who were raised in narcissistic homes can eventually become quite passive because their own thoughts, ideas, and feelings were frequently attacked or dismissed if they varied at all from their parents'. As adults, they tend to be overly compliant to the wishes of their friends, spouses, employers, and children. They will usually struggle with setting boundaries because they weren't allowed to set any growing up. In fact, they learned that setting boundaries actually caused bad things to happen, because if they ever did attempt to say no or disagree with their narcissistic parents, they observed that their parents either quickly withdrew and refused to speak to them for days or weeks, or they were attacked with an annihilating vengeance. Children of narcissists often become what professional therapists call passive-aggressive—since they dared not be aware of or express anger, they learned to suppress it and get vengeance without even knowing they were doing so, passively, by procrastinating, being late, doing tasks inadequately, etc. As adults, they have headaches whenever their mates want sex, "forget" to do things they agreed to do, put down their mates in subtle ways in public in their presence (or behind their backs), and other such passively aggressive (hostile) methods. I (Paul) had one client who reluctantly agreed to paint all the windows in his house and painted them shut! When asked by his wife to hang the Christmas lights on their expensive home, he used huge, ugly nails to do so. He then put off taking the lights down until well into February. He paid his bills late consistently, even though they had plenty of money, thus incurring many late fees and a poor credit rating. This struggle with passivity can create frustration and struggles in marriage and parenting, as we'll see in the following example involving Mike and Christine.

Mike and Christine

Christine married Mike, who came from a narcissistic home. She was often frustrated by Mike's passivity and frequently felt rather abandoned by him because she felt she was left to run the family without much input or help from him. He tended to leave the discipline of their three children to Christine, and he was often viewed as the good guy or the fun one. If Mike was put in the position of being forced to set limits with the kids, he often truly struggled. He had never been taught how to set appropriate boundaries, so he tended to either let the kids run amok or he would be over-controlling of them. He became shocked and very distressed with how willful and disobedient his kids could be. He usually felt very threatened by his children's rebellion and tended to become enraged and reacted with harsh, shaming responses. He was rather shocked by his own behavior, which was inconsistent with his usual passive, amenable self.

Christine explained to Mike that children who aren't terrified of being totally abandoned by their parents will have the audacity to say no. This was completely foreign to him, because this was not allowed during his growing-up years. Mike was very surprised and touched when he would overhear Christine teaching their children how to put their feelings into words, and how to negotiate, compromise, apologize, and express empathy for their siblings' feelings. He was raised to believe he had come from a perfect family, and he actually believed it was Christine's family that had been dysfunctional, because her parents would openly admit their faults and apologize to Christine about the things that they wished had been different during her growing-up years. As Mike came to understand that his family wasn't so perfect, he was able to learn and grow in his own parenting.

Another major issue in Mike and Christine's marriage was the lack of protection Christine felt from Mike as she was often criticized or devalued by her narcissistic in-laws while he didn't seem to even notice. Christine, a bright, articulate woman, shared her thoughts and feelings openly. Mike was so used to his parents' arrogance that he was blind to it. In contrast, his bride was stunned when, whenever her feelings or opinions didn't align with her in-laws', she was either subtly put down or openly verbally attacked by them and told how wrong her beliefs were.

She was stunned that after these tumultuous exchanges, when she would attempt to talk to Mike to explain her hurt feelings, the vulnerable expression of her emotions was usually met with a confused, numb look wherein Mike would show almost no empathy for her plight. He was literally dumbfounded by her reactions. He had learned to deny and suppress his own hurt and anger since the time he was young, and he had lost touch with how painful it felt at times when he had dared disagree with his parents. Mike's reaction (or lack of reaction) would anger Christine, and she would insist that he needed to stand up for her with his family! Again, she was met with more silence and apparent confusion. It finally occurred to Christine that her husband completely emotionally checked out and shut down when he was in the presence of his parents. The best he could offer her during their visits was the unhelpful advice of "Just ignore them," "That is just the way they are," "She [his mother] didn't mean anything by it," "You're being too sensitive," or worse yet, "Why did you have to start a big fight?" Attending some individual and marital sessions at the Meier Clinic brought insight and healing to Mike, Christine, and their family.

A Magnet to Narcissists

Unfortunately, as we said earlier, adults from narcissistic families will often unknowingly choose to be around narcissistic people, because their suppressed feelings of shame and inadequacy will lead them to attach to people that seem powerful, thus helping themselves feel more worthy. In addition, humans are created to deeply imprint their early attachment figures, and what was modeled early on in life is what we take in as normal. I (Paul) learned during my Duke residency that about 85 percent of our adult personality traits are already formed by age six—unless we get therapy or make major choices to change, which most humans do not do.

Therefore, children from narcissistic families will tend to gravitate toward other narcissistically injured children. It is truly all they know. Hence, if the child or teen tends to devalue himself as a result of how he was parented, he will be predisposed to becoming a magnet to narcissistically acting kids. The wounded child, teen, or young adult with narcissist injuries will tend to idealize an egomaniac, as this results in himself feeling more worthy, because he has now attached himself to his new friend's inflated sense of self.

Consequently, the devalued teen will feed the ego of the inflated one. The inflated one will talk despairingly about others and will give the impression that only the chosen will be fortunate to be in his presence. The unspoken message is that if a person falls from his favor, he or she will be cast out and devalued. This puts a kid with a fragile sense of self in a vulnerable position. Often, he will compromise his own wishes and desires (although, often, he is completely numb to feeling or knowing what his own wishes or desires even are—because his family never acknowledged them) and he will, therefore, concede again and again to the wishes and desires of his puffed-up friend.

It is not uncommon for adults raised in narcissistic homes to come into counseling seeking to learn how to make their relationships healthier, only to discover that they have filled their lives with narcissistic spouses, coworkers, friends, bosses, and so on.

Healing for Adult Children of Narcissistic Families Involves:

- We need to admit that going through life denying our feelings and denying who we really are isn't working for us.

- We need to come to understand that even though we were too much for our parents, we can find many people who will appreciate, value, and love us as we really are.

- We must learn to listen carefully to what we say inside ourselves and learn to deny messages that aren't true, healthy, or good for us.

- We must become more aware and honest about how we feel, what we believe, what we want, and what we like and dislike.

- We must learn communication skills, because they were not taught to us growing up. These include how to set boundaries by expressing our feelings to people when they are hurting us or angering us and being able to articulate to them what we want and need and what we will do if they don't listen or respond.

- We need to learn how to negotiate and compromise wherein both peoples' views and feelings are considered, not just one.

- We need to address the issues that have arisen in our lives that have resulted from denying our real selves (perfectionism, being a magnet to narcissists, etc.) and get the help and support we need to address these issues.

- We need to find more safe people in our lives—people we can be real with, people who show us empathy and grace and don't attack and devalue our thoughts and feelings. Safe people will tell us the truth about ourselves when they see us faking it (pretending to be happy when we're upset) or being self-destructive or when we're acting out. Furthermore, safe people allow us to tell them the truth about how we see and feel about them. With safe people, we do not feel as if we are walking on eggshells to avoid rejection or abandonment. We know we do not have to risk losing the relationship if we have a conflict we need to work through with each other.

· We need to grieve that we have lost a lot of time. We have rejected kind people who wanted to love us and we have chosen people who couldn't because of what we believed and how we felt about ourselves (even though we were not often conscious of this).

· We have to face that we married a narcissist or that we have spent years trying to please a narcissistic friend, boss, or family member.

· We need to become willing to deal with how we feel and what we believe about our parents and eventually come to understand that most of the time, people are doing the best they can with what they have been taught from their own experiences; yet, some people truly are cruel and destructive and we need to distance ourselves from them.

· We need to come to understand that, often, we have internalized narcissism, and this leads us to sometimes think and act in narcissistic ways. When we do act self-righteous or overly critical of others, we need to apologize and express empathy for their feelings.

· After we learn, grieve, and grow, for our own good, we need to forgive (without condoning their behavior) the people in our past and present who have hurt us, and we need to forgive ourselves for our own hurtful narcissistic behaviors as we grow more able to love and be loved unconditionally by people who know our real selves—faults and all.

CHAPTER 5

NARCISSISM IN MARRIAGE

People who are married to spouses with narcissistic issues tend to struggle with a mixture of confusing emotions. They feel perplexed, but they're not sure why. They feel like something isn't quite right, but they're not sure what it is. It usually takes them quite a long time to begin to sort out what is truly going on. It often takes years.

Mark and Carla

Carla often feels lonely, but she's not sure why. Things look pretty good to outsiders. She struggles with self-doubt. She has tried so hard, for so long, to make Mark happy. She is becoming exhausted and yet, things don't seem to be getting better. She feels frustrated, because no matter what she does, she can't seem to connect with Mark on a deeper level. Sure, they talk. They talk about the bills, chores, doctor visits, the neighbors. Things seem to go fairly well as long as she supports everything he does—and never shares a differing opinion.

And Carla has certainly learned to not be too vulnerable, not to express too many emotions. When she forgets this and begins sharing her heart with Mark, he often says nothing and then quietly dismisses himself into the next room. He gives no response and acts as if she wasn't speaking. She has learned to not follow him to persist in continuing her conversation, lest she get the look—the look scorning her for being too emotional, too sensitive, too intense, always negative, always going on and on. Or the "Oh no, here you go again" or the "What, are you crazy?" look.

Carla has learned to shut down, because experience has taught her that nothing productive happens once she gets the look. She has come to know that no matter how hard she tries to express her thoughts or her feelings it only gets worse. She only gets further devalued. She is growing hopeless; she is afraid because her energy is running out, and the hours of her lonely days feel endless. She cannot connect with this man. He does not see her. He shows no interest in who she is. He does not care what her thoughts and feelings are, what her hopes and dreams are: not if they vary from his.

Something inside her is fighting or wanting to fight, wanting to scream, "I'm not crazy, I'm not stupid, and you're not always right!" But their fights in the past have gotten them nowhere good, and when the fight is over, while she feels bad and apologizes for the hurtful things she said, he never does, and she is beginning to fear that he never will.

Carla does see some warmth from Mark—toward the dog. He is affectionate with the dog. He even uses a sweet, compassionate voice with the dog. While she once felt like an attractive woman, Carla is beginning to wonder about that. She has rarely received a compliment from Mark over the years, and he's often disinterested in sex. She wonders if it's her. In fact, in the past two years, they haven't had sex at all and have been sleeping in separate bedrooms. She tried to keep their sex life going even though Mark acted so mechanical, never said he loved her, could never look her in her eyes. She even tried to dismiss the pornography she caught him with and tried to ignore his constant flirting with other women in her presence. Their sex life ended when he began having performance problems, and he then withdrew all together. She tried to be supportive and suggested he call the doctor, but he withdrew even further from initiating sex and rebuffed any attempts she made. She finally asked him to move to a separate bedroom, because his emotional coldness and ensuing physical distance became too painful for her.

Sleeping separately feels painful to Carla and it makes the emotional distance in her marriage that much more evident to her. Before, she at least had a warm body next to her at night, even though he felt emotionally cold. She now begins to have some serious concerns about her marriage. Now, she has more alone time to think without Mark present while she is trying to fall asleep at night, and when she is only half-awake in the morning her heart is waking up, her real self is waking up—her self that she has to suppress around Mark or he will devalue her.

Carla's heart is asking her questions: "How did my life become totally centered around pleasing Mark? I had my own dreams, my own life goals. Why have I not pursued them? Oh, because Mark thought it was stupid when I mentioned going back to school. Why did I just completely cave in like that? Oh, because if I disagree with him and try to fight for what I want, he emotionally withdraws even further and won't speak to me for days. Why have I allowed his obnoxious behavior to totally control me? Oh, because I fear he'll leave me. After all, he's always flirting with other women. So, what would be the worst thing about him leaving me? I would feel like a failure. I've tried so hard. I would be so embarrassed. People at church think we have a perfect family, and yet honestly.... I guess I feel so worn out now, and I have a lot of self-doubts. Could I make it on my own? Do I even know who I am anymore?"

What Carla Doesn't Know

What Carla doesn't know is that the reason Mark can't enjoy sex with her is because he is terrified of intimacy. He doesn't want to be that close, that vulnerable. Not with a person who actually knows him. That is too risky. The reason he can't stand it if she has a different opinion is because he has no sense of self. He relies on Carla's affirmations of him to tell him he is a competent, worthy person.

What Carla doesn't know is she can't make him happy, because his unhappiness comes from within. His unhappiness comes from a choice he made in childhood, a choice he was forced to make. He was unable to express his heart to his mother. Mark, like all infants, was born with the desire for deep, loving, abiding attachment. As an infant and a young child, his heart searched for his mother's heart. She was at home with him full-time, yet he could not sense her presence. He longed to be able to make her smile. He longed to be able to feel like he was her pride and joy. But this never happened. She resented his longing for her and felt it was just "one more need, one more demand…one more chore in her unfulfilling life." He came to hate his heart and the needs it conveyed to him. He came to hate all needs. He then built an imaginary world in his head, a world in which he was finally safe. He was safe now because he no longer needed, and he made a vow that he would never need again.

What Mark Doesn't Know

What Mark doesn't know is that extreme anxiety and heightened sexual arousal cannot co-exist. They are mutually exclusive. His anxiety around loving Carla, connecting with her, and expressing his feelings physically and sexually with her were enormously anxiety provoking. This extreme anxiety shut off his feelings of sexual arousal, which then led to a further embarrassing situation. He then felt no sexual arousal and assumed he must lack necessary attraction to Carla. He tried not to say this out loud, but he couldn't stand his feelings of inadequacy. It just had to be her fault. Carla subtly began feeling more and more rejected.

In reality, Mark grew up never feeling adequate enough to please his narcissistic mother. She had unrealistic expectations and was shocked when he couldn't masterfully pull things off. Her scornful looks and emotional withdrawal when she was disappointed in him crushed him. He now has deep fears of Carla. She knows him too well; she has seen him fail. He can't let her get too close, because she will continue to discover his deep inadequacies. He has felt some relief since she requested separate bedrooms. He likes being alone. He's glad the sexual pressure is off. He just can't imagine going through another embarrassing performance failure.

What Now?

There are several factors that positively or negatively determine the outcome of a marriage like Mark and Carla's. One factor is the degree of narcissism in the narcissistically acting spouse with, of course, the prognosis worsening to the degree that the person is more character disordered (with more impairment in being able to see himself realistically, the less able the person is to take responsibility for choices and actions and the less empathy he has toward others' feelings). Also, age can be an important factor. Most of us tend to mellow with age and become slightly less dogmatic about our positions either because we have less energy or perhaps because we've had years of hearing many differing views, and life has forced us to realize that we're not always right and we do fail, and that failure is not going to kill us like we think it will. In fact, as we mature, we often realize that it is often failure that drives us to learn, grow, and mature even more. Abraham Lincoln went through two bankruptcies, the death of his two sons, and lost elections that all molded him into perhaps the greatest president in American history.

It is important to note that the narcissistic spouse will be more motivated to change if he really doesn't want the marriage to end. Unfortunately, some narcissistic spouses would prefer to be alone. The intimacy that marriage offers is just too threatening. And, unfortunately, after receiving too much realistic feedback from their spouses, many narcissists begin emotional or physical affairs with others in an effort to feel totally idealized again in a new relationship.

With regard to the non-narcissistic spouse, there are also several factors that positively or negatively influence the marriage. A huge factor depends on if the non-narcissistic spouse can learn to hold onto his sense of self rather than looking to the narcissistic spouse for validation. Another factor is the amount or degree of other stress factors impacting the non-narcissistic spouse. For instance, if the non-narcissistic spouse suffers from a chronic health issue, she will have less energy and will likely feel less tolerant of the insensitive, selfish behavior from the narcissistic spouse. Other stressors, such as financial, parental, needing to take care of an ill parent, or her own mental health issues (struggles with depression, anxiety, or a history of childhood trauma), can give a person less energy or resilience for dealing with a narcissistic spouse.

There are a few common scenarios for how Mark and Carla's marriage can go from this point. We will explain the potential following outcomes by applying them to Mark and Carla's scenario. Each outcome will be Mark's response to Carla's expression of her feelings as in the dialogue in scenario 1:

Scenario #1

Carla begins individual therapy, she joins a support group (a general support group like Celebrate Recovery [see Referrals and Recommendations] or a specific support group for codependency, or both), or she decides to become more real with a friend who has always been open about her own imperfections, and Carla begins to wonder out loud about what is missing. (We recommend that she do all three of these major efforts toward healing.) The empathy she receives strengthens her sense of self and she becomes more in touch with her real thoughts and feelings rather than keeping them chronically suppressed. She is reassured that she is not crazy or unusual in her desire for a healthier marriage. As she begins feeling stronger, she has more energy to directly talk to Mark about her feelings.

Carla understands that Mark is going to feel threatened when she talks to him and is likely to become defensive. She knows she will have to remain calm and not be as easily dissuaded. She realizes that it will likely go better if she can be reassuring to him at times so he feels less threatened, but she also knows that she can no longer cave in to his thoughts and feelings. She needs to at least hold onto her own thoughts and feelings, even if he makes it difficult for her to express them to him. She needs to be prepared to keep upping the boundaries if needed if he shows no motivation to even listen to her feelings. She knows that there is a risk that he will leave her if he simply can't or won't change. She feels more ready for that alternative now, because what she now consciously knows is that she cannot keep living (or not living) like she has been.

Dialogue:

Carla: Mark, would this be an okay time for us to talk? I have some things that I've become aware of that I'd like to share with you.

Mark: Well, I'm not busy now, but you're not going to go on and on, are you?

Carla: No, because I know exactly what I want to say. (She ignores his devaluing comment for now.)

Mark (He is feeling perplexed and becoming slightly anxious because Carla wasn't shut down by his comment and didn't respond with, "Fine, you don't want to hear my feelings anyway!"): So, go ahead. What did you want to say?

Carla: I realize that I have not felt the freedom to share my thoughts and feelings with you because you get really mad if I don't agree with you, or if I need to share that my feelings are hurt about something you've said or done.

Mark: So, what? You think it's my fault that you can't share your thoughts or feelings?

Carla: I'm not saying it's all your fault, but you have been hard to talk to. When I try, we often end up in big fights or I feel like you punish me by not speaking to me for days. I would like to request that you work on trying to listen and express that you care about my feelings, even if you don't completely agree with my perspective.

Mark: Fine, I'll try to listen. So what have you been holding in for our entire marriage that you feel you so desperately need to tell me?

Carla: Well, this is a good example. Your tone of voice is sarcastic and I feel devalued by the way you said "desperately." I must tell you I do feel desperate, because I know I can't go on like this. I just can't stand being in a marriage where my thoughts and feelings don't count.

Mark: So, what? Are you threatening to divorce me?

Carla: I'm not trying to threaten you with anything. I'm trying to share my feelings with you.

Mark: But, if I don't change, you're out of here?

Carla: Look, Mark. Don't you think it's weird that we've been sleeping in separate bedrooms for two years?

Mark: Sleeping in separate rooms was your choice!

Carla: You're right, because I could no longer stand the pain of lying next to a warm body with so much emotional distance, and it hurt me that you never wanted to have sex anymore. That made me feel rejected and makes me wonder why you don't want to get close to me emotionally or physically.

Something is wrong here, and yes, if we don't fix it, we're just going to keep growing more apart. We often feel divorced to me anyway. I feel like we're living a lie, and I feel too worn out to continue going on like this.

Mark: What would people think?

Carla: Well, if that's all you care about, then you're proving my point, and I don't have the energy to go on pretending everything is perfect.

Mark: No, that's not what I meant. I just can't stand the idea of a divorce.

Carla: I don't want to get divorced either, but I've done everything I can to try to build more intimacy into our marriage, and nothing gets better. Maybe you could talk to the pastor. Or my therapist said she has some really good therapists she refers to.

Mark: OK. Get me the names.

Explanation

Mark's response can be common among men over the age of fifty. According to Dr. Stephen Johnson, narcissism in men often decreases from age forty onward as testosterone levels decrease (personal communication). As testosterone levels decrease, a man's sense of being constantly driven will decrease. This causes him to slow down and pay more attention to what those around him are saying and, thus, feeling. As the years go by, he often becomes more patient, empathic, and better at truly listening to his wife. He becomes more tuned in to her facial expressions as well as her feelings. This is why many adults find themselves rather shocked to see how warm, compassionate, playful, and patient their own fathers are as grandfathers when, as fathers, they were rarely thought of with these adjectives! Therefore, the natural changes that occur with decreasing testosterone levels can help improve narcissistic tendencies in some men.

Scenario #2

Mark responds defensively and tells Carla there is no way he is going to get help, but she sees changes in his behavior. He tries to be more patient and tries to listen. He washes her car and encourages her to take the classes she has wanted to.

Carla perceives Mark's attempts as sweet and can see that he really does care for her, even though he still can't express his feelings.

She knows he feels too threatened to say he's sorry, but she can see that he is by his sweet gestures.

As time goes on, Carla feels more seen, heard, and loved, and eventually, she feels better about sharing a bed together. Sex is still a struggle. She can see that Mark does feel panicky and awkward, but she no longer takes it personally. She has come to understand that too much intimacy threatens him. She has learned to share her heart with her therapist and close female friends.

Explanation

Carla believes that Mark is at least making positive moves. She reasons that some people have physical limitations, whereas Mark's limitations are emotional. She figures that she wouldn't scream at a paraplegic and demand him to get out of his wheelchair and walk. She comes to see that Mark has emotional injuries, which cannot be seen, that make him more limited in his capacity for intimacy, but she loves him and believes he loves her too, and she comes to feel much more content with her life.

Scenario #3

In response to the dialogue in Scenario 1, Mark becomes irate and tells Carla that they're not having sex because he's not attracted to her. He totally shuts down and withdraws. The coldness worsens in their marriage. He begins coming home later and later from work. Carla then finds out Mark is having an affair. She confronts Mark with this. He admits to the affair, says he loves the other woman, and wants a divorce.

Carla is devastated, especially because Mark is so willing to discard her so quickly. She asks again about counseling. He refuses and says it was a mistake that he married her to begin with. He moves in with the other woman within a week.

Explanation

In this third scenario, Mark's degree of narcissism is severe. He feels too threatened to pursue a healthier relationship with Carla. He chose to marry her because she was a good catch—bright, capable, beautiful, easygoing—and she was crazy about him, which made him feel on top of the world. He didn't really love her; rather, he loved the way she made him feel. He doesn't want to hear what she doesn't like about him. He doesn't want to make changes. In reality, he doesn't care all that much about how she feels, not if it's negative. In fact, he reasons that he doesn't like everything about her, either! He begins building a list of all her faults. He then starts complaining about Carla and seeking sympathy from a female co-worker about how miserable he is, and before you know it....

Rather than having to deal with truth and reality, Mark chooses to escape having to look at himself through making a quick exit and starting a new relationship. When this happens, he will most likely blame Carla for the ending of the marriage. Oftentimes, he'll be so convincing that close personal friends, family members, and even their own children will believe his version of why the marriage ended, which could include "She's just a chronically negative person.... I could never make her happy; I don't think anyone could.... Depression runs in her family, but she refused to get help...."

Scenario #4

As Carla attempts to get closer to Mark emotionally, he becomes too threatened and begins attacking her with frequent insults. He tells her she's psycho and that she has no grasp on reality. He continues to withdraw further from her, and when she walks into a room, he refuses to acknowledge her presence. He starts acting extra nice to the kids, even using money to purchase their favor, and subtly puts Carla down in front of them. Before Carla knows it, her teenagers

are looking at her differently. They start discrediting mc
she says and they begin repeating Mark's words, tones
devaluing facial expressions, etc.

Carla realizes from her codependency recovery group .... she
has tolerated Mark's narcissism for years because her father was
narcissistic, and it all felt so familiar. But now, she's angry and
frustrated that she has spent her life trying to please narcissists.
She wants honesty in her relationships. She wants to be able to be
herself. She wants to have the freedom to have her own thoughts,
feelings, and opinions. She is tired of walking on eggshells. She just
can't do it anymore. She can't continue to pretend that everything
is fine. She realizes she wasn't allowed to get angry growing up or
allowed to set boundaries. She wasn't able to state her opinions or
express her feelings. She can't keep living like this—it feels like she's
going crazy. She can't stand his constant distortions of reality, the
hostility, and the silence. She's got to get out.

Carla worries that the kids are acting worse as the tension in the
marriage is growing. She feels she's been acting worse with the kids
herself because she can't stand living in an environment where her
reality is never validated. When Mark is gone on business trips, she
and the kids get along fine. It seems as though even the dog is less
stressed when Mark is gone. When he's gone, Carla can be herself,
and she and the kids can have genuine talks about their feelings
and opinions. Then when Mark comes home, so does the tension,
and the focus becomes on him, his moods, and what he wants.

Carla tells Mark she wants a separation. He becomes irate and
tells her that's fine because he can't stand how chronically negative
she is. He moves in with his sister, withdraws all the money out of
their checking account, and files for divorce. He then calls Carla's
narcissistic father and narcissistic brother and spins an amazing
story about how dysfunctional Carla is. They take his side and begin
calling Carla, haranguing her to get back together with Mark. They
tell her she's making the family look bad. This breaks her heart. She
tries talking to them and it becomes quickly obvious to her that

they can't see or hear her either. She begins screening her calls. She is determined to focus on the healthy relationships she is making and on being there for her kids in healthy ways.

Two Years After a Divorce From a Narcissist

(This is a real letter from the ex-wife of a narcissist who divorced her. This outcome is very common).

"As painful as it is, I do believe I'm better off. I miss having a partner, although I have several circles of close friends. But the best thing of this ordeal is that I have peace in my heart and I feel free. I do still get down and at times ruminate about the good ole days and then a friend of mine will give me a reality check. Just recently, one of my friends who has known me about 7 years, told me how great I look…She reminded me that I was a mess when I was married…stressed out, sinus headaches, hives, etc…. She said my whole demeanor has changed. That was cool.

The kids are hurting though….Tracy [her teenage daughter] is being flown to Mexico this week to be with John [her ex] and his girlfriend. She admitted to me she was dreading the trip…and that her dad ignores her. She used to be his shining star…He showered her with tons of attention after he left me…but since his girlfriend moved in…he hardly even notices Tracy. All the kids have told me they can't tell their dad how they feel…that he is always "right" and that if they try to tell him something he's done, he turns it around to be their fault.

Being married to John was exhausting to say the least… It was a rollercoaster of never ending efforts to try to please a discontent person…never being able to get him to respect me and my opinions."

How Did I End Up Marrying a Narcissist?

This question tends to plague people. They want to know how they could have blown such a major decision in their lives. There are a few common answers to this question. Some people just had really bad luck. They trusted charming narcissists who did not show their true colors until after the wedding. But as we have mentioned in earlier chapters, many people who marry narcissists grew up with narcissism in their own families, so it initially feels rather normal. They have their blinders on, and they are usually attracted to narcissists and find kind and loving people boring to have romantic relationships with.

Also, if a person grows up in a family wherein there is alcoholism, physical or sexual abuse, or severe emotional neglect, he or she will have been forced to go numb emotionally to survive the circumstances. This numbness can make us less alert to healthy warning feelings inside of us. If we are in touch with our feelings and we meet someone who is overtly narcissistic, we will feel put off by their grandiosity, by their bragging, by their tendency to put others down in conversations, and by their haughty tones of voice. It is true that they can be quite charming and engaging initially, but it doesn't take long to figure out that conversations have no true depth to them and instead are boringly superficial.

If we meet someone who is more covertly narcissistic, it will usually take longer to figure out that something is wrong, but as time goes on, we will realize that we are finding ourselves giving in quite often to our new friend's plans, wishes, and ideas, and that when we have tried to assert a differing opinion, our ideas were subtly rebuffed or ignored. When we try to assert that we felt hurt or dismissed, we will see our new friend deny her part and turn the situation around and blame us for her behavior. If we are in touch with our feelings, we will become increasingly concerned. However, if we spent our childhoods forced to tolerate someone else's dysfunctional behavior, then the situation with our new friend will feel completely normal.

So again, it is human nature to gravitate toward the familiar. It gets us into trouble when we are detached from our feelings, because our feelings are the very things we need to warn us when we're in danger or in an unfamiliar situation. Husbands and wives frequently berate themselves in therapy sessions, asking why it took them twenty years to really figure out what was going on in their marriages.

The same answers always exist. They either had a mother or father that was cruel, rejecting, or abandoning (either emotionally or physically), or they were not allowed to express their own thoughts and feelings and they became codependent to a parent who struggled with an addiction to alcoholism, perfectionism, legalism, a mental illness, and so on. Or there was either overt or covert narcissism in one or both of their parents.

When Someone From a Healthy Family Marries a Narcissist

There are men and women who have come from fairly healthy families (we believe there are no perfectly healthy families) who have married narcissists. In many of these scenarios, the narcissist did a quite fabulous job of charming the whole family and didn't show his true colors until after the wedding.

It is important to remember that what a narcissist fears most is intimacy, because he has been hurt in his most intimate relationships (with his parents). Therefore, after the wedding vows are said, and are followed with "until death do us part," sheer panic runs through the veins of the narcissist. He now feels trapped, vulnerable, and overexposed (when you live with someone, you can no longer pretend to have no weakness). It isn't long before his true feelings of inadequacy emerge, because he doesn't know how to fix the dishwasher, he feels criticized when his new wife asks him to pick up his clothes, etc.

Suddenly, his charming smile is gone. He now is silent and moody, has a negative or critical spirit, and becomes more possessive and controlling of his wife and attacks her for the ways in which she is different than he. The young bride is stunned. At first, she tries to work through things with him, and then, when she sees he has no ability to negotiate or compromise, and when he becomes crueler and crueler in his verbal attacks toward her, she will consult with a friend or family member.

When she comes from a non-narcissistic family, her family will offer her and her new husband empathy, support, and often the suggestion of counseling. If her husband's narcissism is severe, he will reject any help or support offered and instead will become more and more inflamed, because his wife's family's intimate, loving acts toward him will further panic him as he has not known empathy, warmth, or compassion during times of struggle, and in some cases, he has never had family members directly confront him about his behavior. He will become more defensive and will continue blaming everything on his wife.

Before too long, the situation usually becomes so inflamed that the wife will need to separate from her husband. This woman is not numb to her feelings, so she feels each devastating verbal blow. She finds herself crying frequently, shaking, and feeling as if she's going crazy. Her health is breaking down. She's never seen anyone completely distort reality and refuse to take any personal responsibility. She learned negotiation and compromise in her family, yet nothing is working with this man. She finds herself feeling numb as the trauma persists. She and her family initially hoped he would be able to look at his part in the marital issues just like his wife was willing to examine her own actions, but they all come to see that this man has no intention of taking any responsibility for his actions.

As the situation persists, it will become evident (if he is on the more character disordered spectrum of narcissism) that this man is incapable of seeing himself in a realistic way. This will become more and more disturbing to the new bride and her family as they hear his accusations of her increase, and his version of what is occurring will become increasingly distorted. In fact, narcissists commonly use projection as a major defense mechanism, wherein the feelings and behaviors they are accusing others of having or doing are actually reflective of what they are thinking or doing, and are not at all accurate with regard to those they are accusing.

Once this young bride is living separately from her husband, she will feel that it is safer to feel the feelings that were beginning to go numb from the ensuing trauma. She will feel more and more terror at the thought of returning to a marriage in which she has been emotionally abused and abandoned. She will simply know that she can't do it. She can't live like that—not if he is showing no signs of being willing to change at all. It is over. She doesn't want to get a divorce, and she's humiliated that it all went south so quickly, but if she envisions herself trying to go back, she starts shaking and crying and her heart screams, "NO!" Her family will support her. They don't know what is wrong with this man. They've never met anyone like him, but they are certain that this is not a safe relationship for their daughter. She will do for herself what she would recommend to any good friend whom she loves.

When someone has been raised in a relatively healthy family and he marries someone who is very narcissistically character disordered, the marriage rarely lasts longer than a year or two. Again, when people haven't been conditioned to be emotionally numb, and when they grow up with their parents modeling negotiation, compromise, and the ability to take responsibility for and apologize for their own mistakes, they find severely narcissistic behavior intolerable. If they have had many healthy friendships and have never undergone having their feelings completely disregarded or attacked, again, this will feel intolerable. These marriages usually only work when the narcissistic spouse is able to see and admit there is a problem and seeks help.

Sometimes, though, non-narcissistic spouses force themselves to remain in these marriages because they find divorce to be an intolerable option. In these situations, the non-narcissistic spouses tend to "get it" that they can't express their feelings, desires, or opinions to their spouses, so they give up trying. In some cases, their hearts shut down altogether, but in other cases, they find people in their lives that they can be their real selves with (such as friends, their own children, other family members, a support group, or a counselor). As we mentioned earlier, narcissism can decrease with age. But unfortunately, sometimes it doesn't.

Advice for the Non-Narcissistic Spouse

When you're interacting, on a daily basis, with someone who acts narcissistic, if you do not keep your support system intact, it is too easy to lose yourself and become entangled in a web of distortions and projections, because narcissistically acting people tend to be engaging and articulate. They also tend to be quite convincing due to their high levels of self-confidence. They are sure you will come to see the errors in your ways as soon as you understand the full picture. Before you know it, you can be talking yourself out of reality, because they seem to make so much sense in their distortions and rationalizations.

Your support system needs to include people that your heart feels safe with, people who have empathy for your feelings so you can slowly come into contact with how you really feel about painful or difficult issues in life. You might find, at first, that you have become or have always been fairly emotionally numb or that you tend to discount or disregard your own feelings. This will improve with time spent around people who truly care about what you think, feel, want, and believe.

Receiving support from others will help give you the reserves needed to be kind, patient, and compassionate. The support will also give you the energy you will need to be firm and assertive as you set healthier boundaries with your spouse.

Helpful Things to Remember When Your Spouse Has Narcissistic Issues:

· Even though he doesn't act like it, he struggles with a lot of fear and anxiety about his self-image, his self-worth, and his performance.

· Even though it doesn't seem like it, you are in a very powerful position in your spouse's eyes, and he is fearful of your criticism, your rejection, and your abandonment of him.

· He believes if he admits his weaknesses to you, you will be disgusted and will use his weaknesses against him to humiliate him and gain power over him.

· In order to have the emotional energy to interact with your spouse, you have to come to know and accept yourself—your own strengths and weaknesses, and your own humanity.

· You need to have healthy people in your life who help you to view yourself realistically so that you will know what is true and untrue about yourself. This will help you hold onto your sense of self when your spouse attempts to attack and devalue your character.

· Remember that when your spouse feels threatened, he will often accuse you of the very things that he is actually struggling with, so when he is verbally attacking you, try to ask yourself, "Could his words actually be more reflective of his own behavior than of mine?" (For example, he might say "You always think you're right!") This will help you become less confused and disoriented. Yet, if he has a good point, acknowledge your error and apologize. Even if he can't own his own behavior yet, he will often learn healthy behavior from you.

· Remember that when your spouse is verbally attacking you, he is often feeling very threatened and overly vulnerable.

· Avoid using "should" or "shouldn't" messages with him, which are parent-to-child messages. Rather, tell him how you feel about what he is doing—give a peer-to-peer message that shows more respect. You have more chance of having him hear your message this way, and you will feel better about yourself if you have made a reasonable attempt to work things out. We have seen numerous narcissistic clients who did change and became wonderful mates and parents after extensive therapy.

· It can help if you reassure him that your intent is not to hurt him. State that you are sharing your perspective and feelings in an attempt to work out the issue with him.

· If he attacks you with belittling comments, state that you can see he is obviously upset and you care about his feelings and perspective, but that he needs to stop the cruel attacks or you will have to discontinue the conversation until you both calm down. (If you say, "…until you calm down," he will believe that you're stating that he is pathetic, weak, and emotionally dramatic and will escalate and devalue you even further.)

· Remember that he is watching you closely. Hold onto your sense of self and set limits with him when he is acting cruel, but don't become cruel back; he will often feel remorse for his bad behavior, even if he doesn't admit it to you. You'll see him soften and begin acting better toward you. If you attack him back with cruelty, his narcissistic defenses will only get more deeply entrenched.

· Know that at times, you are likely to become so traumatized by his emotional cruelty that you do temporarily lose your sense of self. During these times, you will feel stunned, numb, and confused about the reality of his distortions. You will likely struggle with more self-doubt during these times. It will help if you talk to your counselor or a trusted friend whom your real self feels safe with. This will likely help you to feel more grounded again, even though it can sometimes take a few days.

During these times, it is important that you distance yourself emotionally from your spouse, because you are too vulnerable to engage in healthy ways with him.

· If you tolerate his distortions of reality or if you don't set limits against his devaluing comments of you and others, it will ensure that he stays in his narcissistic world, because he really believes himself. If no one disagrees with him, he will assume his views are correct.

· A strong warning: you need to be prepared that if you do confront his distortions, even if you reassure him that you love him and want things to get healthier in your relationship with him, he will either gradually gain insight and improve his behavior, or he will become highly distressed and may exit the marriage, because he cannot face taking in the truth of who he is, imperfections and all.

· If you can remember that he is actually deeply insecure and you give him realistic positive feedback about his strengths and the good things you see in him, it will often comfort his anxious heart and make him more able to tolerate his own imperfections.

· If you can hold onto a realistic picture of your own strengths and weaknesses, this will create a picture of healthy humanity for him.

· In long-term marriages with narcissists (depending on the degree of narcissism), things may slowly get better.

CHAPTER 6

INTERACTING WITH NARCISSISTS YOU DON'T LIVE WITH

After getting this far into the book, you have probably discovered (if you didn't know it already) that you know someone who is narcissistic or who acts fairly narcissistic at times. It could be your parent, an in-law, a relative, a neighbor, a coworker, your boss, a person you go to church with, a long-time friend that you just recently disagreed with for the first time, someone that you have to contend with during the holidays, an ex- spouse you share custody with, your adult son or daughter, or your son-in-law or daughter-in-law. Some of these individuals you can simply choose to not interact with, but oftentimes, it's not that simple. We have seen many occasions wherein someone is put in a position of doing the right thing, such as taking care of their dying narcissistic mother-in-law, having to contend with their narcissistic boss because they can't lose their retirement by changing jobs, or having to work issues out with their neighbor because they don't want to move.

As we discussed earlier, in order to have the emotional energy to interact with people struggling with narcissism, you have to have a strong sense of self—you have to come to know and accept yourself, including your own strengths and weaknesses and your own humanity. We build the capacity to do this when we have shared our authentic self with another person who has shown us love, grace, and acceptance. When we can see ourselves through the eyes of someone who knows the truth of who we really are and loves us anyway, it decreases our fears and our shame regarding our weaknesses. In fact, acknowledging our faults and struggles to each other promotes emotional healing and builds intimacy. Even crying with a friend brings healing and comfort.

When we can view ourselves realistically and come to like ourselves enough anyway, we are less vulnerable to someone else's critical attack of us if they attempt to devalue our sense of worth by shaming us about our mistakes or attack our character flaws. When we hold onto our sense of self (when we remember our sense of worth and who we really are), then, when others try to assassinate our character, we wonder why they are acting so surprised that we have flaws, and we ponder what is wrong with their self-esteem that they feel the need to put us down so much with their cruel words. We might assume that they are having a hard time expressing their feelings of anger or hurt towards us and it is therefore coming out as an attack, or we will question if we have made them feel threatened or attacked by something we have said or done. When we are able to hold onto our sense of self, we don't collapse into a puddle and assume that every word spoken must be true.

Honest feedback from people who love and respect us is a valuable gift. But when people put us down or criticize us to others for jealous or hostile motives, they are using defensive devaluation— the myth that if they devalue us, somehow that makes them more valuable. In reality, the opposite is actually what happens if people criticize us in front of healthy people. While narcissistic people spend much of their time gossiping with other narcissists in an attempt to inflate their own self-worth by putting someone else down, healthy people become quickly suspicious of others who feel the need to talk disparagingly about others!

When we are healthy, we tend to be open to the fact that we may not make everyone happy all the time and that we will need to apologize for the feelings we hurt and the mistakes we make, whether they were intentional or not.

It is also quite refreshing to our souls when others interact with us in these same ways—when they apologize to us because we got our feelings hurt (even if they didn't mean it), or when they listen and care about our feelings and perceptions of things (even when we don't make perfect sense). It helps our hearts when we can negotiate and compromise in relationships and see that we are heard and valued and that someone feels close enough to us to even tell us when they think we're wrong, but they still convey love and grace for us. This is true intimacy. This is a real relationship.

When we are grounded in who we are and we have other healthy relationships, this will help us deal with the not-so-healthy relationships we sometimes need to deal with.

Kate's Adult Relationship With Her Mother

During her session, Kate recounted some memories of still trying to connect with her narcissistic mother in adulthood. She shared how painful it was that her mother was still never able to sustain eye contact with her when she tried to share things about herself or her life. Before she could get out more than a few sentences, her mother would change the subject and begin saying something like, "That reminds me of Susie's daughter. She always did that same thing," and would launch into a long monologue that made Susie's daughter's life sound much more dramatic than what Kate was beginning to mention.

This is very common when you're having a conversation with a narcissist. Within a few sentences, you are likely to be interrupted with, "Oh, well, you think that's bad, you should hear about…!" You are left feeling lonely and bored and as if you don't exist. You don't hear empathic statements like, "Oh, that must have been hard!" There is no emotional connection that makes you feel better about having shared something about yourself or your life.

Fortunately, when Kate came to accept that her mom could not tolerate too much intimacy, she modified how she interacted with her. Instead of sharing her vulnerable heart, she chose to interact with her mom around their common interests, and Kate felt genuine joy when she frequently made her mom laugh with Kate's witty sense of humor.

Anna's Adult Relationship With Her Narcissistic Parents

Anna, at the age of thirty-eight, spent two to three nights a week in her narcissistic parents' home. She worked in the family business, which was located several hours from her own home. Trying to survive her few nights spent there per week could be quite an emotional chore. She struggled to endure the empty, superficial conversations with her parents. Topics usually centered around her parents' overidealization of others (how great her married cousins were doing when she was still painfully single) or the devaluation of others ("That poor dear wearing that outfit at that event. I wouldn't be caught dead in that!").

When her mom asked her questions about her life, it was apparent that she hadn't remembered what Anna had shared with her in the past, which only made Anna feel more unseen and alone.

Viewing things from her adult perspective, it was clearer than ever to Anna that everything centered on her mother's needs. For example, at Christmas, Anna received an extremely expensive crystal bowl from her mom. Anna tried to force a smile on her face and say thank you, but it brought up more pain about her mother not knowing her, because she had made it clear to her mom on many occasions that she didn't like crystal. It was her mother who absolutely adored crystal. (This is an example of how a child is a narcissistic extension of the mother's self—the mother assumes her children's needs and thoughts are the same as her own—and any difference is simply not seen, acknowledged, or tolerated. If the child illuminates the difference, the mother usually reacts with denial, criticism, or devaluation.)

Instead, Anna's heart was overjoyed when she received two music CDs from her brother, because they were from a group she had told her brother that she really liked. She was deeply touched that he had remembered. This made her feel that he could see who she was and what her interests were. Of course, her mother caught on to the difference in her responses to the gifts and exclaimed that she could not understand why Anna would be more excited about two fifteen dollar CDs than a four hundred dollar crystal bowl. Anna responded by saying, "Mother, you are the one who loves crystal." Her mom just couldn't comprehend this and withdrew with obviously hurt feelings.

It is important to add at this point that when someone is truly character disordered, she sometimes really isn't capable of much insight. We find it helpful to imagine the person is paralyzed. Would we become angry and yell at the person, insisting that she force herself to get out of that wheelchair and walk? Of course not. So, when we are counseling adults who are interacting with narcissists, we teach them how to make clarifying statements of who they are and what they need, but to try to do it without tons of anger and frustration, because the narcissistic person is often doing the best she can, given her character limitations and disabilities.

Again, Anna simply clarified with her mother that she wasn't intending to hurt her feelings, and shared that the monetary value of a gift was not what was important to her. Instead, she explained, it was whether the gift reflected that the person could see who she is and what her interests are that mattered to her. Anna's mother couldn't really understand what she was saying, but Anna had conveyed enough empathy that it repaired things enough to where they could at least drop the subject and move on with Christmas.

Therefore, as you can see, depending upon the degree of character disturbance, we sometimes have to grieve our higher expectations that we will be able to get this person to engage in healthy conversations wherein we both listen, take in each other's perspectives, feel empathy for each other, as well as for ourselves, and then come to some healthy resolution, which usually involves some type of negotiation or compromise. In fact, one of the most important things we do as therapists to help our clients is to encourage them to give up on false expectations of change in significant others. We also help our clients to not base their sense of self-worth upon the feedback of narcissists.

I (Paul) have told clients from narcissistic families—hundreds of times—"You know, there are about seven billion people on planet earth, and your mother (or father, or mate, or other significant person) is just one of them. You mom is your egg donor and your dad is your sperm donor. What they think of you is irrelevant. You do not need their acceptance, and demanding it is keeping you depressed and frustrated and lowering your self-esteem. Three thousand years ago, the Psalmist David compassionately taught us that God loves widows and orphans, which I am sure includes psychological widows and orphans ignored by narcissists. David goes on to say in Psalm 68 that 'God takes the lonely and places them in families.' We do need to love and be loved by friends who accept and value us as we are, and they become our new family. Do you need my mother's acceptance to be significant?" They always tell me that they don't. Then I ask them further, "Do I need your mother's acceptance for me to feel significant?" They always reply, "Of course not, Dr. Meier." Then I remind them once more that they do not need their mom's acceptance any more than I do, so they should give up trying to get it and put their self-worth back into their own pockets. I say, "Be your own best friend, and never say anything to yourself that you would not say to your best friend under the same circumstances. Kick those narcissistic mother messages out of your brain."

It will help us to remember that if we are expecting fairly narcissistic people to be able to interact like we wish they would, we are setting ourselves up for chronic pain and disappointment, because while we might be able to have these types of interactions with the healthier people in our lives, these expectations are truly unrealistic for the more severely narcissistic. Hope deferred makes the heart sick, so we need to quit hoping for hopeless things to happen. When we don't need anything from a narcissist, it puts us in a less vulnerable position.

In another interaction with her mother, Anna had made it clear that she needed to return home later that afternoon and would not be staying for dinner that night. Her mother began setting the table and set a place for Anna, too. Anna again clarified that she was not staying for dinner and needed to get going. Her mother didn't acknowledge what Anna said and instead told her what they would be eating.

At this point, Anna had been in therapy for some time, and so, instead of becoming enraged at her mother for disregarding her wishes, and at the same time not becoming numb to her own thoughts and wishes (which would be a collapse of her real self), Anna could simply acknowledge to herself that she could see her mother truly did not want her to leave and was unable to express her own wishes (because that would make her mother feel too vulnerable to rejection, so instead, it felt much safer to use control and manipulation to attempt to get her needs met).

Anna had come to understand that because her mother was also a child of a narcissistic mother, she had been forbidden to express her own wants, needs, desires, and wishes with her mother. So, in this case, when Anna's mom asked again, "Can't you eat a little?" and Anna responded, "No, I'd better be going," to which her mother replied, "What kind of salad dressing would you like on your salad?" Anna decided it wouldn't hurt her to sit and have a bite to eat before she got on the road.

In previous years, before therapy, Anna would have complied with her mother's wishes, but not out of choice. Instead, she would have complied out of the collapse of the self, wherein it is too difficult for the child (and eventually adult) to hold onto what she wants because the pressure is too great and she becomes worn too thin and merely runs out of energy to continue expressing her own needs, wishes, feelings, or opinions.

Now, Anna could see that her mom actually wanted her company, but didn't know how to say, "Gee, I'm sad to see you go. I know you need to get home, but is there anyway I could talk you into staying for a quick bite to eat before you have to go?" Anna's new understanding of her mother gave her more compassion and patience. She also was touched and reassured, because now she could read between the lines and see that her mom really did love her, in her own limited capacity.

Anna was no longer controlled by her mother's guilt and manipulation. She understood that she was under no obligation to comply with her mother, but had her own free choice. She understood that leaving, as she said she would, without giving in to her mother, would also have been a totally appropriate choice.

When you no longer need the acceptance of a narcissist, you can behave maturely with that person, doing whatever you think is right for you, and then you can let go of the outcome.

When You Have Married Into a Narcissistic Family

Many spouses who marry into a narcissistic family become shocked and outraged at the family dynamics. They can't quite believe their eyes and ears as they see their new mother-in-law or father-in-law (or both!) treat their spouse and their spouse's siblings completely differently. One adult child, for example, an only daughter, seems to be chosen as the idealized one in the family. This daughter will be able to do no wrong. If she wrecks a car while drunk, excuses will be made for her, because there truly can be no wrong acknowledged regarding this child. Meanwhile, both of her brothers and their children will be criticized and devalued. This, of course, is what creates narcissism in this daughter (now an adult)—she comes to truly believe in her unique status.

Mike and Christine

Before beginning counseling and coming to understand narcissism, Christine was continually shocked and amazed at her mother-in-law's behavior. It all felt so surreal to Christine, because no one else in Mike's family seemed to think there was anything wrong (including Mike!). Here's what occurred:

Mike and Christine lived around the corner from his narcissistic parents. His siblings and their families also lived nearby. Mike was offered a job that would require him and Christine to relocate to a place that was about seven hours away. They understood that Mike's parents would be upset about their move. They figured that would be a natural reaction, but assumed that his parents would be happy about Mike's new position and would come around to being supportive.

When they made the announcement, Mike's mother, Shirley, and his father, Rick, acted as if nothing was said. They showed no reaction and went on talking about superficial things. Week after week, Shirley continued to call Christine announcing to her any new real estate within a few blocks from Shirley's house and encouraged Christine to call the realtor. Discussion after discussion, Christine tried to reiterate that they would be moving out of the area, but it literally seemed to go in one of Shirley's ears and out the other. Rick acted similarly. Christine was dumbfounded by this. She really didn't know what to make of it. Then, when she and Mike actually moved, his parents were shocked and outraged. It was as if they couldn't compute that their son actually made a decision that was different than what they wanted. It further stunned Christine that Mike's parents acted as if their move was a personal assault against them.

Christine could only assume that they were having a hard time adjusting, but she believed that they would eventually come around after a healthy period of grieving (she still had no idea what she was contending with). In fact, from that day forward and continuing on even seven years later, Mike's parents continually acted as if Mike, Christine, and their three children no longer existed. After their move, whenever Christine tried to share noteworthy news about her children with their grandmother, Shirley would look past Christine, as if she wasn't speaking, and would begin talking to others in the room. Once, when Christine attempted to show her mother-in-law a book her children had made, Shirley literally did not make one positive comment, looked totally disinterested, got up, walked away from the book, and changed the subject.

Then, to make matters worse, Mike's sister, Sharon, stayed enmeshed (unable to separate as a unique individual) with her parents. She and her family not only continued to live around the corner, but Sharon still called her mother every day—sometimes several times a day. While Christine could not get Shirley to acknowledge her own children, Christine never heard the end of things regarding Sharon's kids. Shirley went on and on about how much she adored them, how much she bought them, and how much she babysat them, and prattled on and on about all of their various activities right in front of Mike, Christine, and their children. In contrast, the few times Christine asked Shirley to watch her children, Shirley became adamant that she was way too busy.

Christine was not only angered by how her children were treated, but she couldn't stand watching Mike's parents exalt Sharon and ignore Mike. When Mike came into one of Christine's therapy sessions, he clearly explained that he had learned not to care in his family because he had always been treated as if his needs and opinions didn't matter. This absolutely incensed Christine, who had been convinced by Mike and his family that he had come from the perfect family, unlike her family that was open about everything not being perfect during her growing up years. Christine was enraged by the hypocrisy and was shocked at how she had actually allowed herself to be convinced by all of them that she and her own family were inadequate. (See, we mentioned that narcissists can be very convincing!)

Eventually, after Christine learned about narcissism, her visits with her in-laws went much more smoothly. Her in-laws didn't change much, but incidents that would have previously provoked rage in her no longer did, because she no longer had unrealistic expectations. She found that because of her new understanding, she actually experienced much more compassion for her in-laws. In her report about a recent week-long visit, she stated that the visit began with her father-in-law acting tense, irritable, and aloof within the first five minutes. He confronted Mike with the fact that he had heard from Mike's sister "that you and Christine think that your mother and I don't work when we're visiting you." Mike was confused, but his father was not able to clarify the situation further.

Mike and Christine could only guess that perhaps Christine had commented to Mike's sister, Sharon, that their feelings were sometimes hurt because Mike's parents seemed disinterested in their kids and never offered to babysit them, as they frequently did for Sharon's kids. During their week-long visit, because Mike's dad, Rick, was upset, he refused to acknowledge Christine's presence whenever she walked into the same room, even if she spoke directly to him. The situation went so far that, during one of their first vacation days, while Mike, Christine, their children, and Shirley were in the backyard swimming all day, Rick stayed inside the house—never coming outside to even acknowledge their presence. That afternoon, he then left to go to his office without saying goodbye.

What Christine was so excited about was that she no longer became shocked, hurt, or angry at her father-in-law's rude and insensitive behavior.

Furthermore, as she pointed out the interactions to Mike, she was no longer surprised that he hadn't even noticed his father's unusual behavior. She and Mike were able to have healthy conversations about what was occurring with neither of them feeling defensive, and finally Christine was able to hold onto herself (not take her father-in-law's behavior personally), which then enabled her to interact in a friendly, polite manner. As their week-long visit went on, Mike's father slowly warmed up to Christine and her family, and they had a few positive interactions. Christine, to this day, continues to marvel on how un-upset she was during the visit because of her new understanding about narcissism.

As Christine began explaining the change that had happened within her, she said, "I was able to look at my mother-in-law with eyes of compassion for the first time. It made all the difference in the world knowing that their behavior was to be expected for people in their disconnected states." No longer having the unrealistic expectation that her in-laws would meet her needs of feeling valued and loved freed her up inside to love them as they were.

Things to Keep in Mind When Your Parent or In-Law Is Narcissistic:

· It's important to grieve and come to terms with the reality of your parent's emotional limitations, which means you can't be your real self and don't feel emotionally close or safe in that relationship.

· You need to build relationships with other people in your life who can be emotionally supportive to you.

· Try to visit or call your parent (or in-law) when you feel fairly well-rested and not overly stressed.

· Rehearse what you will say if your parent (or in-law) begins acting out, such as trying to make you feel guilty or pressured, or becoming critical or devaluing of you or one of your family members.

· Be direct about behaviors that feel intolerable to you. For example, ask your child to go play with the dog for a minute and then say to your mom, "Mom, please don't comment on Susie's weight. We are working with her on eating healthy foods." Or you might say, "Mom, your negativity and complaining about how long it has been since I last called is putting a damper on our current conversation, so can we just move on? How is your garden coming along?"

- Give realistic positive feedback when you can, such as praising your mother's garden that she works in tirelessly as she continually tries to make it perfect.

- Your parent (or in-law) will be intolerant of mistakes in herself and others. You can role-model healthy behavior by admitting your own mistakes, showing grace when she makes a mistake, and making healthy statements like, "Well, none of us is perfect."

- Get your needs for validation met by healthy people who can give you positive, realistic feedback. If you take your need for validation to your narcissistic parent (or in-law), you set yourself up to potentially feel crushed.

- Don't overdo your visit. Try to make visits short and sweet— not too short, but not so long that you begin to lose your self or your energy to set needed limits.

When a Narcissistic Parent is Dying

Many of our clients have expressed the extreme anguish they have felt when they have been forced to face the impending death of their narcissistic parents. They often long to connect with their parents in a way that has never been possible. They want to help in ways that their ailing parents won't allow. They become deeply saddened watching their once aggrandized parents no longer able to pretend that they are invincible. It is painful to watch their parents' loss of control and loss of self-respect.

Many clients have reported experiencing a few sweet moments when their narcissistic parents or in-laws were able to take in their love and compassion. Unfortunately, the fear of intimacy often persists throughout the dying process, which can leave them with more feelings of emotional abandonment. This can be quite traumatic, because along with a parent dying, a fantasy is also dying—a fantasy that the parent would change and come through with genuine, unconditional love. The loss of the fantasy is often harder to take than the loss of a narcissistic parent. The child of the narcissist may even feel relieved that the parent, with all his unrealistic expectations, is finally gone, giving a sense of relief and lessened stress. False guilt may result from these healthy feelings of relief.

Relating With Narcissistic Adult Children or Sons - or Daughters - In-Law

Many people come into counseling because of ongoing strife in their relationships with their own adult children or with the spouses their children have married. These situations can be quite painful and very stressful. Usually, there are grandchildren involved. It is often worth the effort to make these relationships as healthy as possible.

Helpful Things to Remember:

· Be an example of someone who is able to admit mistakes and apologizes for them.

· Remember that people with narcissism struggle with intimacy, so your warm attempts to reach out may initially be rejected, but your efforts will usually pay off with time and patience.

· If your attempt to reach out is met with a rebuff, hold onto your sense of self and be clear about how you feel. You may have to say, "Sorry, I wasn't trying to offend you when I offered to help with _____. I was trying to be supportive, because I can see you're really busy. I wasn't saying you couldn't do it by yourself, I just thought it would be easier if you had a little help."

- Set limits against abusive behaviors. For example, you can say, "Look, I know I've obviously upset you and I'm willing to hear why, but not if you're going to call me names," or "... but your tone of voice is condescending and offensive." If the behavior does not stop, say, "We're going to have to talk later when things have calmed down." (If you say, "...until you have calmed down," you will evoke more rage.)

When Your Boss is Narcissistic

It is not unusual to find people who struggle with narcissism in management. Their charm and high confidence levels can be quite appealing, and they can often fairly rapidly move up the ladder in companies. Narcissistic bosses can expect unrealistic hours or tasks from their employees. Sometimes they violate their employees with inappropriate jokes, sexual talk, or sexual gestures—like Steve Carell does in the comedy TV show The Office. (Of course, it's often not funny when it happens in real life.)

Things to Help Your Relationship With a Narcissistic Supervisor Go More Smoothly:

- Remember that trust is a major issue for people who struggle with narcissism. It will help in the long run if your supervisor can see that you have genuinely honest, good intentions toward her and the company.

- If she doesn't view you as a threat, because she can see from experience that you "watch her back," she will likely become very loyal to you.

- She will offend many people in the office, including you. Choose not to engage in gossip. When coworkers are venting, just acknowledge their feelings and say something like, "Yes, Sharon can put her foot in her mouth at times." Do not join others in making her all bad. Keep a realistic view of your supervisor's strengths and weaknesses.

· If she gives you harsh feedback about an error you made, hold onto your sense of self, and own the parts that you believe are true. If you feel your boss is scapegoating you (blaming you for not doing something she didn't ask you to do or telling her supervisor that you didn't do your job in order to cover up a mistake she made), make sure you hold onto reality, wait until you feel calm, strong, and confident, and then ask her if you can speak to her. Say something like, "I'm sorry that I turned my report in late. I will turn the next one in on time. But I am still confused about why it is my fault that the contracts didn't get done, because I don't remember you asking me to do those."

· Try to work things out. Even if your supervisor argues with you, the fact that you pointed out that you see that she falsely accused you will make her less likely to do that same action in the future. She will also come to respect you more because you don't attack her, but you refuse to play games. (Remember, narcissists hate to make mistakes and hate being confronted about things they have done wrong, so they will make behavioral changes to avoid having their behavior confronted.)

· Do not allow verbal abuse. If you do, the narcissist will see nothing wrong with her own behavior, and the behavior will continue and maybe even worsen. Remember that narcissists hate having their bad behavior exposed. Even severe narcissists will likely change bad behavior, even if they aren't capable of much empathy or insight. You can say something like, "Wow, did you really mean that when you called me a 'complete moron' yesterday?"

· Don't allow any sexual talk or gestures that are offensive to you. Simply state, "That makes me uncomfortable when you talk like that," or "…when you touch me like you just did." Remember, while she may seem like she's disregarding your words by responding with, "I was just joking," or "Gee, you can't take a joke?" your confrontation of her inappropriate behavior will not go unnoticed by her, and her desire to never have any of her own weaknesses exposed will likely stop her inappropriate behavior toward you if she knows you will always call her on it.

· Do your job, but do not idealize your boss and become too much of a people pleaser. This will only disgust her, and she'll likely devalue you because you are devaluing yourself.

Narcissistic Coworkers (Including Fellow Board Members, Committee Members, ETC.)

We have all likely been in situations that increasingly become uncomfortable because someone starts bragging a lot; dominating conversations, meetings, etc.; putting other people down behind their backs (including you—when you're not around!); and overly competing for the top person's approval. These situations not only get irritating, but frustration can grow as your plans and projects get delayed, sidetracked, or sabotaged if the narcissist feels threatened by you and begins competing with you.

Things to Remember With a Narcissistic Coworker:

· People with narcissistic issues will tend to be very competitive, because their sense of self is dependent upon how much praise and recognition they receive regarding their performance.

· Offer realistic praise when warranted. This will not only ease your coworker's performance anxiety, but it will also show him that you're not out to beat him (and, eventually, this should decrease his competitiveness with you).

· Hold onto a realistic view of your own strengths and weaknesses so that you don't feel overly threatened when your co-worker compares himself to you.

· If you tell him you don't like his idea, it feels to him as if you're saying you don't like him, because he does not have a solid sense of self.

· When you need to disagree with him, your relationship will go more smoothly if you make it clear that you are not trying to offend him, but you have a different idea, and you have adapted his ideas in the past and want your idea considered this time. Do not be fake or unrealistic with your praise, because he'll distrust you. However, when you legitimately bring up positive feedback, it will help soothe his sense of rejection, and things will likely proceed more smoothly.

Dealing With a Narcissistic Employee

Many business owners and managers have dealt with employee situations that became confusing and tense due to narcissistic issues arising in one (and often in several) employee.

Helpful Advice:

· Remember that your employee is likely to be very sensitive to criticism, but she will work very hard for positive feedback. When you do have to criticize her performance, it will help if you can say something like, "I might not have told you this clearly, but next time in your report, can you include___?" However, be completely honest; don't make things up.

· If expectations are clearly outlined and she receives positive feedback when she is meeting the mark, she will likely be quick to catch on to expectations and to perform to an excellent standard.

- The narcissistic employee is likely to need feedback regarding her interpersonal relationships. For example, you might have to say, "When you're sharing your ideas in our conference meetings, try to be careful to watch your tone of voice. Sometimes you state things so confidently that it can give the impression that you believe that only your way is right. That can make it intimidating for other people to speak up in the meetings."

- She is likely to want you to change the rules. If she suggests something you don't want to adapt, tell her how you see she could want that, but that it's just not possible because of company rules or it would conflict with the bigger picture, etc. Know that she will not take "no" easily and will likely try to persuade you further as her feelings of panic grow, because her sense of self is based upon your validation of her; this makes her feel not as if she has an idea, but as if she is her idea. Try to be patient yet firm. Remind her that you have adapted her other ideas, but this one is just not possible. If she feels heard and respected, she is likely to come around.

- Make it clear to all your employees (so the narcissistic ones don't feel criticized) that if they have a problem with something you've said or done to please come talk directly with you, but not to engage in office gossip, because you want to maintain a positive working environment. (When narcissistic people don't feel heard, they are likely to try to persuade other people to agree with their position because, remember, they are their ideas.)

- As narcissistic employees continually strive for excellence and to be the best, they will often work tireless hours and become genuinely remarkable in their accomplishments. If you give realistic positive feedback, set limits for them by explaining how their behaviors impact others, and give them clear guidelines of how you want them to respond to various situations—and if they don't feel overly criticized or attacked and feel that you genuinely care about them—they will often be worth your time and effort.

- If you have a narcissistic employee that is creating too much havoc and nothing that you try seems to work, if you continue to confront her behavior (and she sees it in writing), and if you tell her that you will need to fire her if her behavior doesn't change, she will likely quit in order to save face.

Narcissistic Friends, Neighbors, and Others

It can be quite unsettling and sometimes even very distressing when we suddenly find ourselves in a huge conflict with a friend, a neighbor, a family member, or someone else we care about. Tension or issues sometimes build over time. Other times, conflict can seem to erupt out of the blue.

Often, these eruptions occur when one or the other of us has felt criticized or put down in some way. It is natural that our feelings will be hurt and we will feel offended when someone we care about insults us. Sometimes the person meant to insult us, but oftentimes words are said carelessly or are misunderstood, or were said in reaction to our hurting the other person's feelings or offending her in some way. Many of these relational rifts can be mended if we take a few healthy steps. First, it is a good idea for us to wait until we are calm. We can then go back to the person and apologize for anything we knowingly did that was hurtful. We can tell our friend, neighbor, or whomever that we felt hurt, offended, put down, etc. when she said _____ or did _____. If she becomes defensive (which is common), we can say, "I totally get it that you didn't mean to hurt me, but I wanted to tell you how I am feeling so we can move on." We can then apologize for any ways she tells us that we unknowingly hurt or offended her.

The closer we get to people and the more time we spend with them, the more likely we are to have misunderstandings and temporary rifts. We actually grow closer to people after we have been able to work through conflicts with them wherein we were each able to show the other compassion and respect. We are relieved when we find that we can work through things in our relationships, because we know that we can't expect ourselves to be perfect and to never blow it during times of stress, being over-tired, and under other such conditions.

However, in a particular relationship, if you feel chronically unseen and unheard and feel the other person is not able to empathize with your feelings or your views in situations, or if you frequently feel the person is competing with you, you are likely dealing with someone with narcissistic tendencies. Depending upon the circumstances, you can choose how much contact you want or don't want to have with this person. When you do have contact, it may help if you keep a few things in mind:

Help With Narcissistic, Friends, Neighbors, and Others:

- Remember that even though the person may seem puffed up, he actually struggles with deep insecurities. Giving him realistic positive feedback will hopefully decrease his insecurities, as well as his need to compete with you.

- Hold onto a realistic view of yourself and don't allow his view of you to define you. You will be able to do this if you are spending time with other people who don't need you to agree with them and who don't feel the need to compete with you.

- Set an example of not having to be right, but when you disagree, if he keeps trying to tell you that you are wrong, make an assertive statement that you believe you are both entitled to your view of things and don't always have to agree, but can still like and respect each other. (This may be a brand new concept for him because that wasn't his experience in his family.)

- If you have had an argument, after you feel calmer, tell him that you did not intend to offend him, and apologize for anything hurtful you said. If you feel you were offended by something he said, tell him what it was and how you felt. He will likely become defensive. Reiterate that you understand that you know he didn't mean to offend you or you know he was mad when he said what he said, but tell him that you'd like him to apologize for his part as you apologized for your part, so that no resentments will build in your relationship. If he begins blaming his behavior on you, assertively tell him that you know you had a part in things, but that you both need to take responsibility and apologize for your parts so you can move on.

- Remember that he fears that if he admits his weaknesses to you, you will use his weaknesses against him to humiliate and gain power over him. It will likely calm his anxiety if you reiterate that you care about your friendship with him and just want to be able to move forward in a healthy way.

- If the person is not willing to repair the rift without continually making you all bad, then it is not a healthy relationship. You will need to decide how much time and effort you want to put into this relationship without causing emotional damage to you.

CHAPTER 7

WHERE TO GO FROM HERE

As we said in the introduction, we believe that it is a rare person who intentionally sets out to destroy his own life or the lives of the people he loves. We continually see in ourselves and others that we all tend to repeat the same patterns until we become more conscious of what the problems are. However, even then, we still often don't change much until we know how and what to change. Human nature is complicated and so are relationships. Change often takes time. It also takes a lot of forethought, effort, patience, and room for quite a few mistakes.

We wrote this book because we believe in the process of change. As we said earlier, some of us will take longer than others to change, and some of us will need therapy to change, but if we want to change, we can change. Narcissistic character traits are common. What we see is that the more we are able to recognize and address these characteristics in ourselves and in others, the more unstuck our lives and relationships become. Furthermore, as we build safe people into our lives who love us as we really are and who also lovingly tell us the truth about ourselves, we not only become healthier, but we eventually become happier and more content. We come to view ourselves realistically and we don't hate ourselves for our struggles and defects. This gives us more confidence as we relate with others both personally and professionally.

We find it helpful to keep in mind the questions listed in the Narcissistic Traits Questionnaire. The most important question we can ask ourselves is, "Am I viewing myself or acting as if I am superior or inferior to the person I am currently with?" When we ask this question and the other questions of ourselves and others, we can quickly gain the insight we need about whether narcissism is interfering in our relationships.

Remember that if you are interacting on a daily basis or even fairly frequently with someone who acts narcissistic, you really need to build a good support network of safe people who can give you the empathy and support you will need. This will help give you emotional energy to share your feelings and set boundaries with the more narcissistic individuals in your life. Healthy people will also help you with accountability if you start to wear down and become emotionally abusive (or narcissistic) yourself. They will remind you of how to get your point across in a healthy manner. We all need the support, empathy, and accountability that healthy relationships with safe people bring. Humans were never created to go without needing others. The messages we receive or have received that we are not supposed to need others are narcissistic messages.

When we are healthy, we understand that we will not make everyone happy all the time, but we will listen to and show empathy for their feelings. We will apologize for the feelings we hurt and the mistakes we make whether they were intentional or not.

It will give us hope and energy for life as we build more healthy people into our lives who can interact with us in these same ways— people who apologize to us because our feelings were hurt (even if they didn't mean to) and listen and care about our feelings and perceptions of things (even when we don't make perfect sense). It will comfort our hearts when we can negotiate and compromise in relationships and can see that we are heard and valued. We will also come to deeply appreciate those in our lives who feel close enough to us to even tell us when they think we are wrong, but they still convey love and compassion for us. This is true intimacy. This is a real relationship. Becoming more real in our relationships with ourselves and with others will greatly increase our happiness and contentment in our lives.

Referrals and Recommendations

Meier Clinics: 1-888-7-CLINIC or www.meierclinics.com. Has counseling clinics in many states and can give referrals for all states.

Free Recovery Groups

Celebrate Recovery: www.celebraterecovery.com. Offers groups to help men and women "...break free from their hurts, hang-ups, and habits".

Co-Dependents Anonymous: www.coda.org. Offers groups "...for men and women whose common purpose is to develop healthy relationships".

Website Help

www.NarcissismCured.com

Recommended Readings

Beattie, Melody. Beyond Codependency: And Getting Better All the Time. Center City, MN: Hazelden Foundation, 1989.

Beattie, Melody. Codependent No More. Center City, MN: Hazelden Foundation, 1987, 1992.

Beattie, Melody. The Language of Letting Go (Hazelden Meditation Series). Center City, MN: Hazelden Foundation, 1990.

Cloud, Henry and John Townsend. Boundaries Face to Face: How to Have That Difficult Conversation You've Been Avoiding. Grand Rapids, MI: Zondervan, 2003.

Cloud, Henry and John Townsend. Boundaries in Marriage. Grand Rapids, MI: Zondervan Publishing House, 1999.

Cloud, Henry and John Townsend. Changes That Heal: How to Understand the Past to Ensure a Healthier Future. Grand Rapids, MI: Zondervan, 1990, 1992.

Cloud, Henry and John Townsend. Safe People: How to Find Relationships that Are Good for You and Avoid Those That Aren't. Grand Rapids, MI: Zondervan, 1995.

Hemfelt, Robert, Frank Minirth, and Paul Meier. Love Is a Choice: The Definitive Book on Letting Go of Unhealthy Relationships. Nashville, TN: Thomas Nelson, Inc., 1989.

Townsend, John. Loving People: How to Love and Be Loved. Nashville, TN: Thomas Nelson, 2007.

References

Johnson, Stephen M. Character Styles. New York: W.W. Norton, 1994.

Millon, Theodore. Disorders of Personality: DSM-IV and Beyond. New York: Wiley, 1996.

About the Authors

Paul Meier, M.D. is a psychiatrist at the Meier Clinics in Richardson, Texas and is the author of more than eighty books, including Love Is a Choice, Happiness Is a Choice, Blue Genes, and Everything I Learned Since I Knew It All. He has appeared on hundreds of radio and television programs over the past thirty years, including shows with Oprah, Tom Snyder, Norman Vincent Peale, Joyce Meyer, Sheila Walsh, Paula White, and many others. He is also the founder of the national chain of counseling clinics called the Meier Clinics, a non-profit corporation (visit www.paulmeiermd.com and www.meierclinics.org).

Lisa Charlebois, M.S.W., L.C.S.W. was the director and a staff therapist at the Meier Clinics for fourteen years and is now in private practice in Gold River, California. She and her husband, Danny, have three teens and live in Orangevale, California.

Cynthia Munz, M.S., L.M.F.T. became a Licensed Marriage and Family Therapist after completing her first career as a mom and homemaker. She was a staff therapist at the Meier Clinics for twelve years and is now in private practice in Placerville, California, where she lives with her husband, Eric.

To contact Lisa or Cynthia, visit www.youmightbeanarcissistif.com.